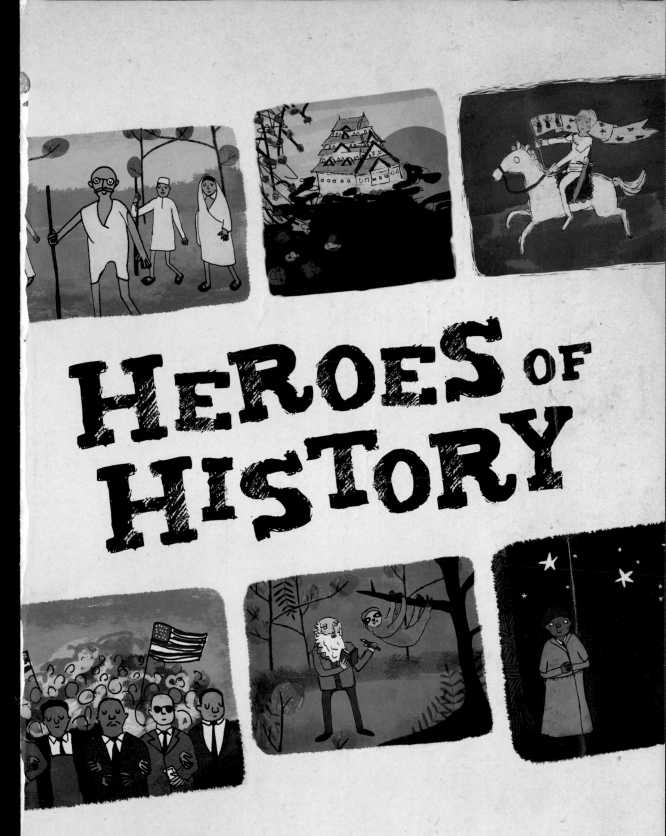

HeRoeS of HISTORY

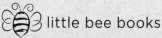

little bee books

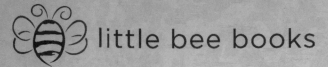

little bee books

An imprint of Bonnier Publishing Group
853 Broadway, New York, New York 10003

Created by:
    Author: Anita Ganeri
    Additional text: Nicola Barber
    Illustrations: Joe Tood Stanton, Kate Abey
    Editorial: Hannah Wilson, Lydia Halliday
    Senior Designer: Krina Patel
    Designer: Natasha Rees
    Index: Vanessa Bird

Manufactured in China (025)

Printed in Guang Dong, China

First Edition 10 9 8 7 6 5 4 3 2 1

ISBN 978-1-4998-0079-1

www.littlebeebooks.com

www.bonnierpublishing.com

HEROES OF HISTORY

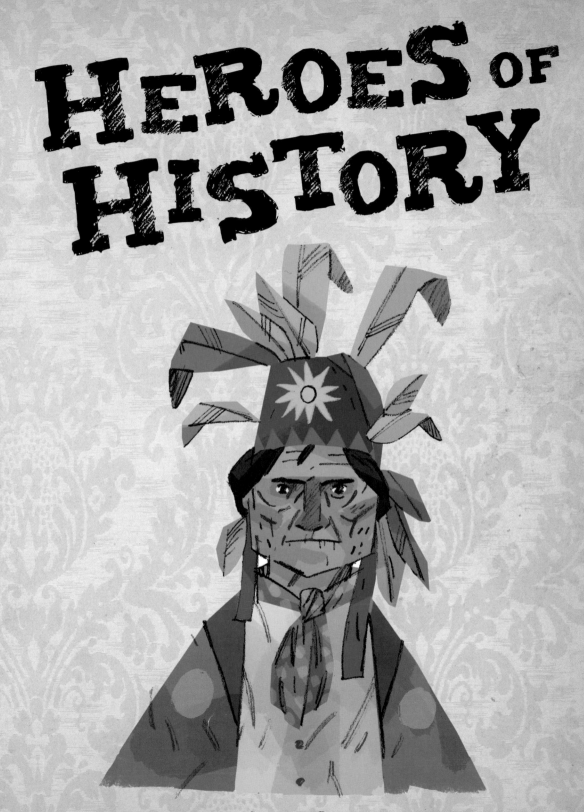

by **Anita Ganeri**
illustrated by **Joe Todd Stanton**

CONTENTS

CHAPTER 5
INNOVATORS

CHAPTER 6
TRAIL BLAZERS

INTRuDUCTIuN

Which dashing knight had his life saved by a humble loaf of bread?

Which daring explorer became the first human to reach the South Pole?

Who rose from being a soldier to becoming the first US President?

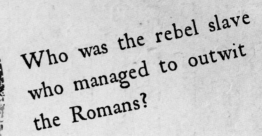

Who was the rebel slave who managed to outwit the Romans?

Which famous scientist was the first woman to win a Nobel Prize?

History is packed with heroes and heroines who left a lasting legacy behind. Some were larger-than-life characters, born leaders who inspired their followers. Others worked away quietly, shunning the limelight. They earned their fame in different ways—through hard work, determination, and sometimes, sheer luck.

CHAPTER I
WARRIORS

Throughout history, great warriors have found themselves pitted against each other in bitter battles and conflicts. With bravery and self-sacrifice, they have faced danger, disaster, and even death. Some warriors have fought in armies, guarding their lords or kings, bound together by codes of loyalty, courage, and respect.

Sir William Marshal

Joan of Arc

Some fought to defend their beliefs, often against huge odds, while others battled for the freedom of their people or country. Many did not fear death as long as it was honorable.

In this chapter, you can read about a dashing knight famous for his fighting skills and chivalry, a brave fighter who gave up her life for her faith, a Samurai from a humble home who became a great hero, and an Apache who suffered a terrible tragedy and vowed to take his revenge.

Saigo Takamori

Geronimo

Sir William Marshal

Medieval Knight

In medieval times, knights were gallant soldiers, bound by a code of chivalry to fight for their country and protect their king or lord. Among them was William Marshal, who rose from humble beginnings to become the greatest knight Europe had ever seen.

Early life

Born in 1146, William Marshal had an unbelievable start to life. As a young boy, he was taken hostage by King Stephen of England to force William's father (who was fighting for Stephen's rival, Queen Matilda) to surrender his castle. The king threatened to have William hanged if his father did not obey. But his threat did not work. So King Stephen ordered his men to launch William from a trebuchet (giant catapult). But in the end he could not bring himself to harm the boy.

Becoming a knight

William's father was a nobleman, but because William was not the eldest son and had no lands or fortune to inherit, he had to make his own way in life. It was decided that he would become a knight. At the age of 12, he was sent to Normandy in France to be brought up in the household of William de Tancarville (his mother's cousin). Here, he began his training, learning not only swordsmanship and riding, but also Latin, chivalry, and how to cope with the politics of a life at court.

William was knighted in 1166 while on campaign in Normandy. His first experience of battle is said to have been a success. According to reports, William fought bravely, but he did not manage to seize any loot or hostages to ransom off. For a knight, making a profit was just as important as fighting with honor. But he was soon to find his real talent in life—winning tournaments.

SIR WILL'S KNIGHTLY DIARY

Sometime in 1167
Normandy, France
A brilliant day! Lord William took me to my first tournament. I won everything, including most of the battles (which were as deadly as the real thing). And this time, I remembered to take the losing knights hostage, so I made a bunch of money ransoming them off with their horses and armor. This is definitely the life for me.

Summer 1168
Poitiers, France
Things haven't been going so well lately. In March, my lord was killed in a skirmish, and I was taken prisoner. I had a wound in my leg that turned nasty. Luckily, someone took pity on me and sent me some bandages, hidden inside a loaf of bread. That saved my life. Anyway, eventually the ransom was paid by Queen Eleanor of Aquitaine—apparently, she'd been impressed by my bravery.

A day in August 1189
Tower of London, England

My wedding day! My new wife, Isabel de Clare, is beautiful, kind . . . and really, really rich. Her father is the Earl of Pembroke, and he's given us several large estates as wedding presents. I'm going to be one of the wealthiest men in the kingdom—who'd have thought it? Now we've just got to decide which one of our (many) castles we should live in.

June 15, 1215
Runnymede, England

For the last few years, I've been mostly in France, negotiating on behalf of King John. Then King John and I fell out big time (long story). Anyway, I'm back in favor, and I'm here at Runnymede to witness the sealing of the Magna Carta. It's a charter setting out new laws that everyone, including the king, has to obey—let's see how that turns out.

November 11, 1216
Gloucester, England

King John died in October, and I organized his funeral and burial in Worcester Cathedral. A sad day. Today, I was named as regent for his son, King Henry II. He's only nine years old, so he needs some help ruling the kingdom. A very great honor indeed.

MILITARY LEADERS

Sir William Marshal had all the best qualities of a knight. Like many knights, he was a skilled horseman and a fierce fighter, but he was also brave and loyal.

Engraving of a medieval English knight

The greatest knight

William Marshal, the son of a nobleman of little importance, ended up as regent—effectively the ruler of England. At the age of 70, he led the king's army into battle and victory over the rebellious barons. After his death in 1219, he was called the "greatest knight that ever lived."

William the Conquerer

William became Duke of Normandy (in France) as a young boy and grew up to be a skilled knight. In 1066, he invaded England and won the Battle of Hastings. William was crowned king of England on Christmas Day.

Bayeux Tapestry showing Norman invasion

Statue of Díaz on his horse, Babieca

Rodrigo Díaz de Vivar

Rodrigo Díaz de Vivar, a nobleman from Castile, northern Spain, became commander of the royal troops at an early age. Later, he became military leader for the Muslim rulers of Zaragoza—a kingdom in northeastern Spain. He conquered the kingdom of Valencia, ruling it until his death in 1099.

Timeline of medieval army commanders

1066
William the Conquerer
French duke wins the Battle of Hastings
and becomes King William I of England.

1094
Rodrigo Díaz de Vivar
Castilian nobleman, nicknamed El Cid
(meaning "the Lord"), conquers Valencia.

1191
Richard the Lionheart
English king joins the Third Crusade, a
campaign to seize control of the Holy Land,
an area now part of the Middle East.

1217
Sir William Marshal
At the age of 70, leads the king's army
to victory at the Battle of Lincoln.

1242
Alexander Nevsky
Prince of Novgorod (now part of Russia) conquers the
Germans in the Battle on the Ice, fought on a frozen lake.

JuAn of ArC

Faith Fighter

The Hundred Years' War between France and England lasted from 1337 to 1453. The soldiers were fighting for control of France. Among them was an unlikely heroine—a young girl named Joan, who claimed that God had sent her to save France.

War-torn times

At the time of Joan's birth on January 6, 1412, the Hundred Years' War had already been raging for seventy-five years. At stake was the question of which country— England or France—had the right to the French crown. Nearly all of the fighting had taken place in France as a series of wars, with short periods of peace in between. By now, the French army had not won any major victories for many years, and the English had the upper hand.

Joan, the daughter of a farmer, was born in the village of Domrémy in northeastern France. She did not learn to read or write, but her mother took her to church and taught her about her Christian faith, which became a guiding light in Joan's life.

During Joan's childhood, her village was attacked several times—and even set on fire—but it still remained loyal to the French crown. Then, in 1420, the French queen, Catherine of Valois, signed a peace treaty, disinheriting her son Charles (later Charles VII) and making the English king, Henry V, ruler of both England and France.

His young son, Henry VI, succeeded him in 1422. England occupied much of northern France, and many people in Joan's village were forced to flee. Then, one day, Joan's life changed forever, and with it the fate of France.

JOAN OF ARC'S ORLÉANS DIARY

One day in 1425
Domrémy, France
An amazing thing has happened. I was in the garden when three figures appeared in front of me. I knew them from pictures in church—they were St. Michael, St. Catherine, and St. Margaret, sent to me by God! I cried because they were so beautiful. They told me that I must save France by helping to drive out the English and making Prince Charles king. Then they were gone. I still can't believe it.

Sometime in early 1429
Orléans, France
I'm here at the royal court, though getting here wasn't easy. I had to crop my hair and put on boys' clothes so no one knew I was a girl because there's a stupid rule that says only boys are allowed to fight. Then I had to cross enemy territory, which took 11 days. I knew Charles as soon as I saw him and told him he would be crowned soon. I also told him that God wanted me to lead an army to Orléans, which is under seige from the English. And guess what? He agreed!

May 8, 1429
Orléans, France

It's over. The siege is over after five long months. The turning point came yesterday. I rode into battle, carrying my banner, but an arrow hit me in the shoulder and I had to turn back. I came back later for another assault and we were able to capture the English fortress. After this, the English left in a hurry. I'm being called a hero, but this is all God's work.

July 17, 1429
Reims, France

The day we've all been waiting for—Prince Charles's coronation in the cathedral. He is now officially King Charles VII of France. Long live the king!

Spring 1430
Rouen Castle, France

I'm being kept prisoner by the English. While we were defending Compiègne, I was thrown from my horse and captured. They tell me they're putting me on trial for witchcraft and heresy, among many other things. I've been trying to get a message to the king, but so far he's not replied. I spend my days praying—only God can help me now.

DETERMINED DEVOTEES

Joan of Arc believed that she had been called by God to go into battle. Many other people throughout history have been prepared to lay down their lives for the sake of their faith.

Statue of Joan of Arc

Joan the saint

Joan of Arc was put on trial by the English, accused of being a witch, of heresy, and of dressing like a man. King Charles could not help a possible witch, and so Joan was found guilty. On May 30, 1431, she was burned to death at the stake. Joan was made a Catholic saint in 1920.

Thomas Becket

Thomas Becket worked for the Archbishop of Canterbury and became friends with King Henry II. In 1161, Henry made Becket archbishop. But Becket argued with the king and stood up for the Church. In 1170, he was murdered.

Cathedral window honoring Becket

Syrian banknote depicting Saladin

Saladin

Saladin was the sultan of Egypt and Syria and the founder of the Ayyubid dynasty, which ruled much of the Middle East in the late 1100s and 1200s. A devoted Muslim, Saladin conquered the Christian Crusaders in 1187 to retake Jerusalem. Saladin gave much of his money to the poor.

Timeline of faith fighters

1099
Godfrey of Bouillon
Medieval knight becomes Defender of the Holy Sepulchre
after the capture of Jerusalem during the First Crusade.

1170
Thomas Becket
Murdered in Canterbury Cathedral
after opposing King Henry II.

1187
Saladin
Muslim leader recaptures Jerusalem from the Crusaders
after a famous victory at the Battle of Hattin.

1430
Joan of Arc
Captured by the English, accused of witchcraft,
and burnt at the stake one year later.

1535
Thomas More
Beheaded for treason for opposing King Henry
VIII's separation from the Catholic Church.

SAIGO TAKAMORI

Samurai

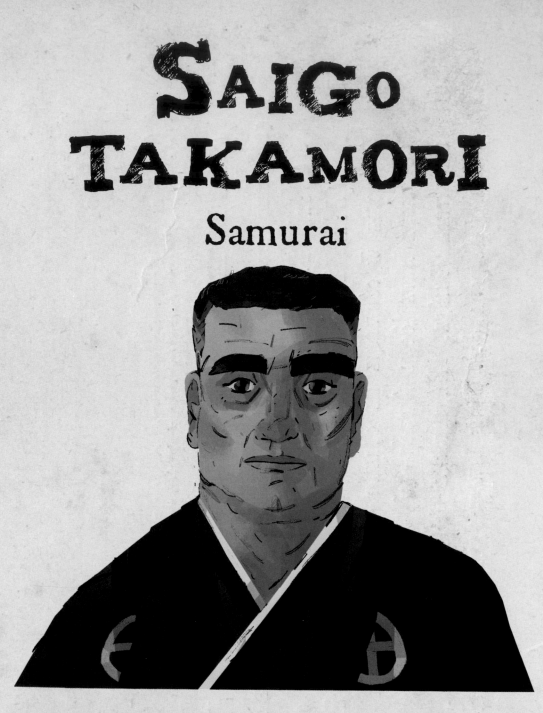

As traditional Japanese warriors, the Samurai were bound by a strict code of honor—Bushidō, or "Way of the Warrior." The code valued loyalty, bravery, and respect—all virtues that Saigo Takamori, known as the Last Samurai, possessed in abundance.

Early life

Saigo was born on January 23, 1828, in Kagoshima, Japan. His father was a low-ranking Samurai, so the family was poor and only just managed to scrape by. Saigo and his six younger brothers and sisters shared one blanket at night, and his parents had to borrow money to buy land to grow food for the family.

At the age of six, Saigo was sent to the local Samurai school, where he was given his first sword. It was his first step on the road to becoming a great warrior, though he preferred reading to practicing sword-fighting. Saigo left school at the age of 14, and went into the service of the local daimyo (lord). Some time later, he got married, but tragedy was not far off. Both of his parents died within months of each other, leaving Saigo head of a large family with very little money to support them.

Promotion and exile

At work, Saigo's talents were quickly recognized, and he was promoted to the post of the daimyo's attendant. Together, they traveled to Edo, the capital of the shogun (military ruler), where Saigo became the daimyo's closest advisor. He secretly helped the lord to plot with his allies to put the emperor back in power, at the expense of the shogun.

On July 16, 1858, the daimyo died suddenly, and Saigo found his life in danger as the shogun threatened to kill anyone who had supported the emperor. Saigo fled to Kagoshima, but the new daimyo would not protect him. Rather than face arrest, Saigo went into exile on a small island. There, he got married again, had a son, and carved out a new life for himself.

SAIGO'S SAMURAI DIARY

February 1864
Kyoto, Japan

What an exciting few years! There I was, in exile, when I was suddenly called back to Kyoto and offered a position in the emperor's court. It didn't last long. I soon fell on the wrong side of the new daimyo and was banished to a small island. Again. Worse was to come. I was moved to an even smaller island—basically a lump of rock in the sea—where I stayed for a year. Anyway, I'm back now, in Kyoto, where I've been appointed Commander of the Imperial Army. No one is more surprised than me.

April 4, 1868
Edo, Japan

A great day. After weeks of hard fighting, the shogun (who doesn't want the emperor back in power) has surrendered. Phew! After a fierce battle at Toba-Fushimi, we beat him back to Edo and had him surrounded, so he didn't have much choice. But I'm glad it's over. We allowed him to keep his head—there's already been enough bloodshed.

October 1873
Kagoshima, Japan

That's it—I've resigned. I've had enough of all the fighting. I'm retiring to the country to play with my kids and go fishing. The final straw was the business with Korea. The Koreans wouldn't accept the emperor as, well, the emperor, and this was a terrible insult to Japan. The government wouldn't invade Korea despite this. I tried to persuade them that it was a reason to go to war—but no one took a blind bit of notice. Now, where's my fishing rod . . . ?

February 1877
Kumamoto Castle, near Kagoshima

Well, that didn't last for long. I'm holed up in Kumamoto Castle with an army of rebel Samurai. We didn't like the way the government was taking away our privileges—including stopping us from carrying swords—so I was asked to lead a protest against the government. To be honest, it's not going that well. We're massively outnumbered by the emperor's army, and we're running short of supplies.

September 23, 1877
Shiroyama mountain, near Kagoshima

We can't go on much longer. There are only 300 of us left, and tomorrow we go into battle against 7,000 imperial troops. I'm not afraid of dying, as long as I die an honorable death. That is the way of the Samurai.

BRAVE WARRIORS

Saigo died at the Battle of Shiroyama, but his reputation as a legendary hero lived on in Japan. Like other great warriors in history, he is remembered for his bravery and skill.

Statue of Saigo in Tokyo, Japan

The last samurai

The Battle of Shiroyama was the last stand for the Samurai rebels. During the attack, Saigo was seriously wounded, so one of his servants beheaded him—giving him a Samurai's honorable death. Saigo is known today as the "Last Samurai."

Alexander the Great

At age 20, Alexander became king of Macedonia and began conquering territories that were under the rule of the Persian Empire. By 331 BCE, he controlled a huge empire that extended from the Adriatic Sea to the Indus River.

Alexander in battle

Stamp depicting Zenobia

Zenobia

Zenobia became queen of the Palmyrene Empire (based in Syria) in 267 CE and led her armies to conquer Egypt. But when the Roman emperor defeated the Palmyreans, Zenobia was taken to Rome. No one knows what happened to her, and the rest of her life remains a mystery.

Timeline of skilled fighters

336 BCE
Alexander the Great
Takes the throne in Macedonia and becomes
one of the greatest military commanders in history.

269 CE
Zenobia
Queen of the Palmyrene Empire challenges
Roman rule in Egypt.

1013
Sweyn Forkbeard
Viking king of Denmark becomes
the first Danish king of England.

1071
Alp Arslan
"Courageous Lion" and second sultan of the Seljuk Empire
defeats the Byzantines at the Battle of Manzikert.

1877
Saigo Takamori
Dies an honorable Samurai death
at the Battle of Shiroyama.

GERONIMO

Apache Attacker

It used to be traditional for skydivers and paratroopers to shout "GERONIMO!" as they jumped out of an airplane to show that they were not afraid. But who was the real-life Geronimo, and why would calling his name help a person to feel brave?

The early years

Geronimo was born in June 1829 near Turkey Creek, a branch of the Gila River in the modern-day state of Arizona. Back then, Arizona was part of Mexico. His grandfather, Mahko, had been chief of the Chiricahua Apache tribe. Named "Goyahkla" ("one who yawns") by his parents, he would later gain fame as Geronimo, the greatest Apache warrior of all time.

Young Geronimo dreamed of the day when he would become a great warrior. He practiced his warrior skills with his friends, fighting mock battles and hiding from the enemy, knowing that one day their lives might depend on these skills. Meanwhile, he worked as a farmer, helping his father to raise their crops. It was a traditional Apache upbringing. Geronimo and his family lived in a home made from antelope and deer hides. As soon as Geronimo could handle a bow and arrow, he began to hunt small animals.

A young fighter is born

At age 17, Geronimo joined the council of warriors, which meant that he could now go into battle. He also earned the right to marry. He had fallen in love with a beautiful girl named Alope. Soon they married, settled down, and had three children. But his life was about to change forever.

Tension was growing between the Apache and the Mexicans, who accused the Apache of raiding their towns. The Mexican leader, Colonel José María Carrasco, believed that all of the Apache were robbers and murderers. He vowed to take revenge. In March 1851, while Geronimo and the other Apache men were away, he ordered his men to attack the camp where their families lived.

GERONIMO'S APACHE DIARY

March 5, 1858
Kas-ki-yeh, New Mexico

The worst day. We were camping near Kas-ki-yeh. I went into town with the other men to trade. On our way back, we met some people who told us that the Mexicans had attacked our camp. We split up and hid until nightfall when we crept into the camp. Dead bodies lay everywhere, among them my mother, wife, and three little children. From this day on, I vow to get my revenge on the Mexicans, however long it might take and whatever the cost.

Sometime in 1873
Casa Grande, New Mexico

I always knew the Mexicans were a rotten lot, but this time they've gone too far. We were exhausted after months of fighting and so agreed to meet them at Casa Grande to sign a peace treaty. All went well until the Mexicans gave us a drink to celebrate, and we all got horribly drunk. Then they killed twenty Apache and captured many more. Peace? Pah! Dirty double-crossers.

Sometime in 1876
San Carlos, Arizona

Yes, we're back at the San Carlos Reservation. Those pesky US troops keep rounding us up and bringing us back, as if we're cattle. Anyway, it'll give us time to get more warriors together and to trade for new guns and ammunition. Then those Mexicans had better watch out!

Sometime in 1880
Robledo Mountains, New Mexico

Hah! That showed them. We escaped from the reservation, but the soldiers came after us, so we hid in a cave in the mountains. They waited outside to catch us . . . and waited, and waited, and waited. While they were waiting, we snuck out through a secret exit and escaped! They were furious when they found out— serves them right!

September 4, 1886
Skeleton Canyon, Arizona

Another bad day. After years of giving the US authorities the slip, we finally got caught. We just ran out of places to run. I, the great Geronimo, surrendered. There was nothing else I could do! We were taken prisoner and sent to Fort Sam Houston, then to Fort Pickens. They're setting us to work sawing logs, but that won't stop us. No way!

INDEPENDENCE FIGHTERS

After his death, Geronimo's name became linked with daring and courage—it even became the motto of a US army parachute regiment. Other rebels are also remembered for their bravery.

Photograph of Geronimo taken in 1903

Celebrity and death

In his old age, Geronimo was famous, taking part in many wild west shows, but he was never allowed to return to the land of his birth. In February 1909, he fell from his horse and died a few weeks later. On his deathbed, he confessed that he regretted surrendering in 1886.

Boudica

In 60 CE, Boudica, queen of the Iceni, a tribe of eastern England, led a rebellion against the Romans, who had conquered southern Britain. She destroyed Colchester, St. Albans, and London before being defeated.

Statue of Boudica in London

Nanjing's city gate, built under Zhu's rule

Zhu Yuanzhang

Zhu Yuanzhang joined a monastery at a young age. When it was destroyed by Yuan troops, Zhu joined a rebel group fighting to overthrow the ruling Yuan Dynasty, and he soon became a commander. He conquered Nanjing, and in 1368, proclaimed himself emperor of China.

Timeline of bold rebels

60 CE
Boudica
Queen of the Iceni tribe leads a revolt
against the Romans in Britain.

1297
William Wallace
Scottish landowner leads a rebellion against the English
king and wins a famous victory at Stirling Bridge.

1368
Zhu Yuanzhang
Becomes the first emperor of China's Ming Dynasty.

1813
Simón Bolívar
Venezuelan statesman begins to lead Venezuela, Colombia,
Ecuador, Peru, and Bolivia to independence.

1886
Geronimo
Apache warrior surrenders to US authorities.

CHAPTER 2
EXPLORERS

For centuries, intrepid men and women have risked their lives to explore far-reaching parts of the world, and go farther, higher, and deeper than anyone has before. Some traveled for money, voyaging far and wide to open up the world for trade. Others wanted to spread their religious beliefs or find new lands to settle in.

Roald Amundsen

Sir Walter Raleigh

Many were scientists and geographers, curious to see and map the world. Others were in it for adventure—they wanted to head into the unknown simply because it was there.

In this chapter, you can read about a sly sailor who set off to search for gold, a gritty explorer who became the first to reach the South Pole, a fearless female flying ace who mysteriously disappeared, and a pair of daring divers who plunged into the deepest part of the ocean.

Don Walsh & Jacques Piccard

Amelia Earhart

Sir Walter Raleigh

Gold-digger

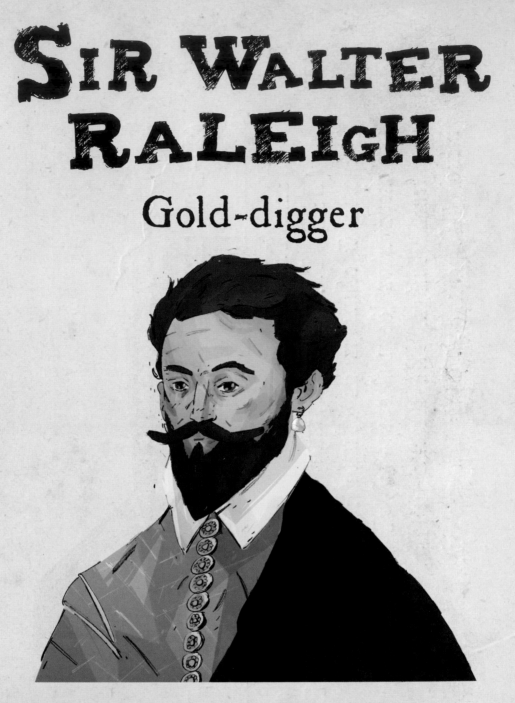

Explorer, poet, and courtier, Walter Raleigh became a firm favorite of Queen Elizabeth I—until he crossed her by marrying someone else. Famous for his daring voyages, he helped to found the first British colony in America, and he led the search for the lost city of gold.

Early life

Raleigh was born in Devon, England, into a wealthy family. He had five older brothers. For a time, he attended Oxford University, studied law in London, and also served in the army in France. His actions earned him a large gift of land in Ireland, where he lived for many years.

In 1578, Raleigh sailed to America with his half-brother, the explorer Sir Humphrey Gilbert, and formed a plan to set up an English colony there. Later, he provided the money for a colony at Roanoke (in modern North Carolina), but the colony failed, as did a second settlement. Raleigh is said to have brought potatoes and tobacco back to England from his travels.

Serving the queen

In 1581, Raleigh returned to England from Ireland, and took up a place at court. He quickly caught the eye of Queen Elizabeth I, who knighted him and made him captain of the Queen's Guard. But his fortunes were about to change.

In 1592, the queen discovered that Raleigh had secretly married one of her ladies-in-waiting, Bess Throckmorton. Furious, she ordered Raleigh to be put in prison, and Bess to be dismissed from court. Both were thrown into the Tower of London, though Raleigh was released after a few months. Now, he needed to win back the queen's favor, and he had a cunning plan—he'd lead an expedition to locate the legendary city of El Dorado, famed for its dazzling wealth. It was rumored to lie somewhere beyond the Orinoco River in Guiana (modern-day Venezuela). What could possibly go wrong?

RALEIGH'S EL DORADO DIARY

March 1595
The Atlantic Ocean

The queen finally gave me the go-ahead to search for El Dorado (she doesn't want the Spanish getting there first), and last month we set out from England with five ships. The crowds waved and cheered, and our spirits were high. Big mistake! The journey has been disastrous so far—we've already lost two of our ships.

May 1595
Trinidad

After forty-six days at sea, we landed on the island of Trinidad, which was controlled by the Spanish, and captured the town of San José. We also took the governor prisoner. He's spent years searching for El Dorado himself, so I figured he'd be useful. Far from it. True, he told me all he knew, but his main advice was . . . DO NOT GO!

June 1595
Orinoco River, Guiana

I should have listened. Here's what happened. I took 100 men over to the mainland, and we set off up the river by raft. It was tough going against the current, and we kept getting swept off-course. Not to mention the mosquitoes eating us alive. We found a few (small) gold mines, but then it started to rain . . . and rain . . . and rain. The river has turned into a torrent, and I've given the order to turn back. So, all we've got to show is a bag of rocks and some miners' tools—the queen is not going to be happy.

June 1617
Orinoco River (again)

Well, I'm off again, but it hasn't all been plain sailing. King James I stuck me in the Tower for 14 years, then suddenly, last year, he had a change of heart. Actually, he's running short of cash and he needs me to find him some gold, and fast.

April 1618
Atlantic Ocean

What a disaster! I got sick and I couldn't lead the expedition, so I sent my son Wat instead. I gave him strict orders (from the king himself) not to upset the Spanish. He completely ignored me—he attacked San Tome, a Spanish settlement— and ended up being shot dead. I'm on my way home now, in disgrace (again). I guess it'll be back to the Tower for me.

WORLD EXPLORERS

Sir Walter Raleigh was one of many explorers who have set out to far-off lands in search of fame and fortune. Their adventures made for great stories, but they didn't all have happy endings. . . .

Sir Walter Raleigh

Sentenced to death

Raleigh was arrested on his return to England. The Spanish were furious about the raid on Tome, and the king was furious that Raleigh had come back with no gold. He was executed on October 29, 1618. Many people considered his execution unjust, and he became a popular hero.

Marco Polo

In 1271, Marco Polo, a merchant from Italy, traveled to China and other parts of Asia. He was away for more than 23 years. Polo wrote a book about his journey—the story was so amazing most people thought it was fiction!

Marco Polo on an Italian banknote

Italian explorer Christopher Columbus

Christopher Columbus

Born in Italy, Columbus, an experienced merchant sailor, proposed sailing westward to find a new route to the "East Indies." His fleet set out in 1492 and landed in the present-day Bahamas, which he claimed for Spain. Columbus made two more voyages to the "New World."

Timeline of great voyagers

1271
Marco Polo
Venetian merchant sets off to Asia,
spending seventeen years in China.

1492
Christopher Columbus
Sails westward across the
Atlantic to the "New World."

1520
Hernán Cortés
Spanish conquistador (conqueror)
defeats the Aztecs of Mexico.

1521
Ferdinand Magellan
Portuguese explorer dies, but in 1522, one of his ships
completes the first circumnavigation of the globe.

1595
Walter Raleigh
Sets sail for the city of El Dorado in
Guiana (modern-day Venezuela).

ROALD AMUNDSEN

Polar Explorer

In the early twentieth century, pioneering polar explorers set their sights on reaching the South Pole. They included British Captain Robert Falcon Scott and Norwegian explorer Roald Amundsen. But who would get there first? The race for the Pole was on. . . .

Budding explorer

Amundsen was born in Borge, Norway, on July 16, 1872. His family were shipowners with strong ties to the sea. Amundsen's mother wanted him to become a doctor, and he dutifully went off to study medicine. But he'd always dreamed of being an explorer, and when his mother died, he promptly left university for a life at sea.

In 1899, Amundsen sailed to Antarctica for the first time. Unfortunately, his ship got stuck in the ice, and the crew had to spend the winter there. Four years later, he led an expedition to the Arctic, becoming the first to sail the Northwest Passage between the Atlantic and Pacific Oceans.

A change of plan

Amundsen was busy planning his next trip—to the North Pole—when he heard that Americans Frederick Cook and Robert Peary had beaten him to it. Instead, he set sail for Antarctica on June 3, 1910, aboard his trusty ship, *Fram*. Not everyone was happy—Captain Scott was already on his way south. The first he knew about Amundsen's expedition was a telegram: "BEG TO INFORM YOU FRAM PROCEEDING ANTARCTIC — AMUNDSEN."

Six months after leaving Norway, *Fram* reached the Bay of Whales on the Ross Ice Shelf. Amundsen and his men spent the winter gathering food and supplies for their journey ahead. Finally, in October, everything was ready. Amundsen set off with four companions, fifty-two dogs, and four sleds full of supplies.

AMUNDSEN'S POLAR DIARY

October 22, 1911
Ross Ice Shelf, Antarctica

We set off from base camp three days ago, and the weather has been terrible—much colder than expected and with steady snow. Thick fog made it tough to see, and my sled, with me on board, nearly fell into a crevasse when the snow bridge broke underneath us.

November 17, 1911
Transantarctic Mountains

Amazing news! We've reached the Transantarctic Mountains, so we're halfway there.

We've been making great progress, covering about 17 miles each day. The weather's been good, and the dogs are running well. Now we've got to get through the mountains, but I think I've found a route up the glacier so it shouldn't take too long.

November 21, 1911
Butchers' Shop Axel Heiberg Glacier

I take it back. It took us three grueling days to climb the glacier, and we kept having to change course because the snow was so soft and deep. Anyway, the good news is we're on the Polar Plateau. The bad news is we had to shoot half the dogs for food. It was horrible—we'd grown very fond of them.

December 8, 1911
Polar Plateau

After days of terrible blizzards (we spent four days holed up in our tents), things are looking up. We've passed Shackleton's farthest-south record, and the sun is shining. We can't be far from the Pole now—just one last push.

December 14, 1911
The South Pole

We've made it—
we're the first
people to reach
the South Pole!
We planted the
Norwegian flag in
the snow. There
wasn't any sign
of Scott, but we
pitched a tent and
left him some
supplies. We also left a letter for him to deliver
to the King of Norway in case we don't make it back.

POLAR EXPLORERS

Amundsen announced his South Pole success in March 1912. By then, Scott had also reached the South Pole—only to find that he'd been beaten to it. Other polar explorers made similar strides.

Statues of Amundsen and his team

To the North Pole

In 1918, Amundsen sailed through the Northeast Passage of the Arctic aboard his new ship, *Maud.* Then in an airship in 1926, he completed the first verified flight over the North Pole. In 1928, Amundsen's plane disappeared on an Arctic mission to look for survivors of an airship disaster.

Sir Ernest Shackleton

In 1915, Shackleton's ship, *Endurance,* was trapped in ice in Antarctica. Shackleton and five others sailed a small boat 807 miles across the treacherous Southern Ocean to South Georgia. A rescue party found the entire crew.

Ernest Shackleton depicted on a stamp

Explorers traveling across the Arctic

Ann Bancroft

In 1986, American Ann Bancroft reached the North Pole after fifty-six days of walking and pulling dogsleds. When she journeyed to the South Pole in 1993, she became the first woman to have stood at both poles. In 2001, she and Norwegian explorer Liv Arensen skied across Antarctica.

Timeline of polar adventurers

1909
Robert Peary
American explorer claims to
reach the geographic North Pole.

1909
Ernest Shackleton
Leads his team to make the first ascent of
Mount Erebus, a volcano in Antarctica.

1911
Roald Amundsen
Becomes the first person to
lead a team to the South Pole.

1912
Captain Robert Falcon Scott
British Royal Navy officer reaches the South Pole,
but he and his companions die on the return journey.

1986
Ann Bancroft
First woman to reach the North
Pole, and in 1993, the South Pole.

AMELIA EARHART

High-flier

By the time of her death in 1937, Amelia Earhart was one of the most famous women in the world. The first woman to fly over the Atlantic Ocean, she had become a role model to millions. But how did she become a pilot in the days when most flying was done by men?

Childhood games

Amelia was born in her grandparents' house in Atchison, Kansas, on July 24, 1897. She moved many times as a child because her father often changed jobs. From a young age, Amelia was a daredevil. She loved to play outside, climb trees, hunt rats with a rifle, and go sledding. One summer, her father took her to a fair where she saw a roller coaster. Back home, she built her own in the back yard. The first run ended in a crash landing, but Amelia didn't care. It was just like flying, she said.

The flying bug

After leaving school, Amelia spent Christmas with her sister in Toronto, Canada. World War I was raging, and the hospitals were full of wounded soldiers. Amelia volunteered as a Red Cross nurse. It was difficult and tiring work, but despite the long hours, she still had fun. One day, she and a friend visited an airshow and watched a flying display by a World World I ace. The pilot spotted Amelia and her friend and dove straight at them. Instead of being frightened, Amelia was thrilled—she knew she had to fly.

In December 1920, Amelia took her first flight. It lasted for only ten minutes, but it changed her life. A few weeks later, she had her first flying lesson. Her teacher was Neta Snook, one of the very few women pilots. Amelia was a fast learner. She quickly took the plane up into the air, and later that year she made her first solo flight.

AMELIA'S AERONAUTICAL DIARY

May 15, 1923
California, USA

I finally got my pilot's license—I'm only the 16th woman to have one. I've already bought my first (second-hand) plane. It's bright yellow so I've nicknamed it the *Canary*. I also bought myself a leather flying jacket—I slept in it for three nights to make it look "lived-in." And I cut my hair short. Reckon I look the part now.

June 18, 1928
Burry Port, Wales

I'm so excited! We've just landed off the coast of Wales after an epic flight from Newfoundland in Canada. It's taken us twenty-one hours, but we're here, safe and sound. My job was to keep the flight log, but it still makes me the first woman to fly the Atlantic Ocean!

May 20, 1932
Culmore, Northern Ireland
After the Atlantic flight, things went crazy. Suddenly, I was famous and everyone wanted my autograph. I wrote a book, gave lectures and speeches, and got married! But I really wanted to set a record of my own. So this time I've flown solo aross the Atlantic. It took about fourteen hours, and it was pretty windy and icy at times. But here I am in Ireland—yippee!

March 20, 1937
Ford Island, USA
It's so frustrating! I've been planning this around-the-world flight for a year now and everything seemed to be in place. I had a plane specially built, but things keep going wrong. I set off from Oakland

three days ago with my navigator Fred, but we ended up here for repairs. Then, when we were taking off again, one of the tires blew, and the flight was called off.

July 2, 1937
Lae, New Guinea
Good news! The plane was repaired, and we took off in May, flying east along the coast of South America and across the Atlantic to Africa and Asia. We got here a few days ago and are set to head off to Howland Island, about 2,500 miles away. It's a tiny island in the middle of the Pacific, so it's going to be tough to find.

HIGH FLIERS

The twentieth century was a time of many notable "firsts" in flight, as humans learned to make aircrafts that could take them higher, faster, and farther. Amelia Earhart was just one of the many pioneers who risked her life to push the boundaries of flight.

Earhart in the plane in which she disappeared

Amelia disappears

In July 1937, Amelia Earhart and her navigator Fred Noonan struggled to find Howland Island in cloudy conditions. Their radio messages became fainter and then stopped. Nobody knows if the pair died when their plane crashed into the sea or if they landed elsewhere and became castaways.

Otto Lilienthal

German Lilienthal was fascinated with the idea of human flight. He made gliders, some with flapping, bird-like wings, others like biplanes. He completed about 2,000 short flights between 1891 and 1896, until he died in a glider crash.

Otto Lilienthal, "the father of flight"

Wright Brothers National Memorial, USA

Wright Brothers

Brothers Wilbur and Orville Wright were busy running a printing works and a bicycle repair shop in Ohio, USA, when they read about Lilienthal's death. They decided to build their own flying machine. In December 1903, the Wright Flyer made the first successful engine-powered flight.

Timeline of famous pilots

1896
Otto Lilienthal
German pioneer completes about 2,000 short
glider flights by this time.

1903
Wilbur and Orville Wright
American brothers succeed in inventing and flying
the first plane.

1927
Charles Lindbergh
US aviator makes the first nonstop
transatlantic flight from New York to Paris.

1928
Amelia Earhart
American aviator becomes first woman to complete a
flight across the Atlantic ocean.

1947
Chuck Yeager
US pilot becomes the first pilot
to break the sound barrier.

Don Walsh & Jacques Piccard

Deep-sea Divers

The mighty Mariana Trench is a massive slash in the Pacific Ocean, near the Mariana Islands to the east of China and Japan. It is about 1,584 miles long and reaches a maximum depth of about seven miles, making it the deepest place on planet Earth.

Building a bathyscaphe

Jacques Piccard was born in Belgium on July 28, 1922. His father, Auguste, was an inventor and explorer who had set altitude records in a hot-air balloon he'd designed. When Auguste started work on a bathyscaphe (like a mini-submarine, for exploring the deep sea), Jacques left his job as a university lecturer to help him . . . and never looked back.

Luckily for the Piccards, the US Navy was so impressed by the bathyscaphe, called *Trieste,* that they bought it and hired Jacques as a consultant. The plan was to eventually use it for underwater rescue and salvage, and the Navy began testing the craft on deeper and deeper dives.

Teamwork

But Jacques had an even more daring dive in mind—a voyage to the bottom of the sea, something no one had ever attempted before. For this adventure, Piccard teamed up with US Navy officer Lieutenant Don Walsh, an experienced oceanographer who had spent many years at sea, mostly in submarines. He also worked in research and development for the Navy—the perfect person to be Piccard's co-pilot for this extraordinary challenge.

The site chosen for the descent was the Challenger Deep, a small slot-shaped valley in the floor of the Mariana Trench. It was named after the British ship, *HMS Challenger,* which made the first recordings of its depth in the late nineteenth century. The deepest spot known on Earth, it had never been explored before.

PICCARD'S DEEP-SEA DIARY

January 23, 1960, daybreak
Pacific Ocean
We've reached the dive spot at last after a stormy few days of towing *Trieste* into place. Unfortunately, the sea has been rough, and a few of the instruments have broken. The engineer is making the final checks, then we'll know if we can still dive.
He's just given us the thumbs up—we're good to go.

January 23, 1960, 8:23 a.m.
Pacific Ocean
Don and I climbed into the cabin (it's really cramped and we're perched on stools), and the dive began. At first, everything was calm, but soon we were descending slowly into the pitch dark, and it got very cold. We put on some extra clothes and settled down to wait. The pressure of the water outside is enormous—let's hope *Trieste* can stand the strain.

January 23, 1960, 1:06 p.m.
Challenger Deep
It's taken nearly five hours, but we've reached the bottom! We got a bit of a shock when a window cracked, but we've made it in one piece. We switched on the floodlights and peeked out of the porthole straight at a small white flatfish, a bit like a sole. No one knew anything could live this far down, but then, no one's ever been here before.

January 23, 1960, 4:56 p.m.
Challenger Deep
We spent twenty minutes on the seabed, munching on candy bars and taking temperature measurements. Then we released the ballast (two tons of iron pellets) and began our slow, steady ascent, breaking the surface just before 5 p.m. We've dived to a depth of almost seven miles—deeper than anyone else. Ever. It's going take a while to sink in!

February 1960
Washington, D.C., USA
Since the dive, life has been crazy. We were splashed across the newspapers, and everyone wants to know what it was like there. Now, we're at the White House, being awarded the Legion of Merit by President Dwight D. Eisenhower. What a day!

DEEP-SEA DIVERS

Deep-sea divers are fascinated with the undersea world. Here you can find out about others who have developed new technology to allow them to explore the depths of Earth's oceans.

Stamp depicting bathyscaphe *Trieste*

The adventures continue

In 2012, Don Walsh oversaw the second manned dive to the bottom of the Mariana Trench. Film-maker James Cameron completed the trip in submersible *Deepsea Challenger*. In 1999, Piccard's son, Bertrand, was the first to circle the globe non-stop in a hot-air balloon.

Jacques Cousteau

French naval officer Cousteau experimented with underwater film-making during World War II. He co-developed the Aqualung—a scuba apparatus for divers. In 1950, he set out on the first of many expeditions on his research ship, *Calypso*.

Cousteau's submarine, built in 1966

National Geographic Society, USA

Sylvia Earle

In 1970, Sylvia Earle led a team of women in the Tektite habitat—an underwater laboratory where the scientists lived and worked for two weeks. In 1979, she set a new diving record by walking on the seabed in a special pressurized suit 1,250 feet below the surface.

Timeline of undersea explorers

1934
William Beebe
US explorer becomes the first to make deep dives in the bathysphere.

1956
Jacques Cousteau
Wins a Palme d'Or at the Cannes Film Festival for his documentary film *The Silent World.*

1960
Jacques Piccard and Don Walsh
Make the first dive into the deepest part of the world's oceans.

1970
Sylvia Earle
The first woman to become chief scientist of US National Oceanic and Atmospheric Administration.

2012
James Cameron
Canadian film director and deep-sea diver reaches the bottom of the Mariana Trench.

CHAPTER 3
RULERS

History has been shaped by many powerful rulers, leading their country and people in good times and bad. Some were born into power; others grabbed it for themselves. Some have become famous for leading by example, in battle and in peacetime, often at great personal cost. Some have had the gift of being able to inspire their people to great things.

Elizabeth I

Ramesses II

Others have left a long-lasting legacy, in the form of great buildings and monuments, which ensure that their memory never fades.

In this chapter, you can read about a warrior-pharaoh famous for his temples and tombs, a queen who proved to be one of England's toughest rulers, a soldier sworn in as the first president of the USA, and an army officer who created a mighty empire.

Napoleon Bonaparte

George Washington

RAMESSES II

Mighty King

Ramesses II came to the throne of ancient Egypt at the age of 25 and reigned for an astonishing sixty-seven years. During this time, he fought many battles, founded a new capital city, and built many temples, including the world-famous Abu Simbel.

Ready to rule

Ramesses was born around 1303 BCE. From a young age, he was prepared for his role as king by his father, Seti I. Ramesses accompanied his father when he went on campaigns and was made a captain in the army when he was only 10 years old. He probably did not lead any troops into battle, but he went on to become the greatest warrior-pharaoh that Egypt had ever seen.

A long reign

Early on in his reign, Ramesses built a new capital city for himself close to where he was born and raised in the Nile Delta, the area surrounding the mouth of the Nile River. The city, called Pi-Ramesses ("House of Ramesses"), was famous for its beautiful gardens, orchards, and canals. From here, Ramesses had a handy base for waging war against Egypt's enemies, for leading daring expeditions to win back territories lost by his father, and for securing Egypt's borders.

One of Ramesses's toughest struggles was against the Hittite people, who had built up a great empire in Syria. Ramesses wanted to expand Egypt's borders into Syria, while the Hittites were determined to protect any threat to their trade routes. Things came to a head in 1274 BCE, when Ramesses's mighty army met the forces of the Hittite king, Muwatallis, at the Hittite stronghold of Kadesh. . . .

RAMESSES'S EGYPTIAN DIARY

1274 BCE
Kadesh, Syria
We reached Kadesh after a long march and began setting up camp. Two spies told us that the main Hittite army was miles away, so I'd taken only a small guard with me. I should NEVER have listened. In fact, the Hittites were hiding in the city and took us by surprise. We were heavily outnumbered, but fortunately reinforcements arrived in the nick of time and saved the day! Sort of. Both sides are claiming to have won, but we're in no state to fight it out again.

About 1259 BCE
Luxor, Egypt
I've finally found time to start work on a grand temple, dedicated to, er, myself (well, there's no point waiting until I'm dead). I'm having the pylons (gateways) and walls decorated with scenes from the Battle of Kadesh, showing us winning a great victory over those pesky Hittites. Hah.

About 1258 BCE
Kadesh

I can hardly believe it. After years of fighting, we're finally signing a peace treaty with the Hittites. King Hattusili sent diplomats with the terms inscribed on a silver tablet. I haven't read it all yet, but

there are lots of pledges about living in peace and not invading each other's lands. Let's see. For now, I'm having it carved on the walls of my temple at Karnak—at least it shows I'm willing.

1255 BCE
Abu Simbel, Nubia

The queen (Nefertari) and I are here in Nubia for the opening of my new temple at Abu Simbel. It's my biggest and best building project yet. Actually, there are two temples—one for me and one for the queen. Outside my temple, there are four massive statues of me sitting on a throne, carved out of the rock. Pretty awesome, if I do say so myself.

1250 BCE
Valley of the Queens, Thebes

A very sad day indeed—Nefertari has died. We'd been married for years, and I used to call her "the one for whom the sun shines." We've brought her body to the Valley of the Queens, where she'll be buried in the grandest tomb money can buy. I've had the walls painted with scenes from the Book of the Dead—only the best for her.

POWERFUL KINGS

The reign of Ramesses II (1279–1213 BCE) was the second longest in Egyptian history. He was a popular, powerful king. Find out here about other mighty kings who made their mark in history.

Statue of Ramesses II in Luxor, Egypt

Temple builder

Ramesses's reign marked the peak of Egyptian power and prosperity. He spent a huge amount of Egypt's wealth on building projects. He constructed temples, palaces, and monuments all across Egypt and Nubia. After his death in 1213 BCE, he was buried in the Valley of the Kings at Luxor.

Louis XIV

Louis XIV succeeded his father at the age of four. His young life was marred by unrest, which left him fearful of rebellion. He set up court at his lavish new palace in Versailles, outside Paris, and ruled with absolute power.

Statue of Louis XIV at Versailles, France

Zulu shield, spear, and club

Shaka Zulu

Shaka, the son of a Zulu chieftain, took power of the Zulu kingdom in South Africa after his father's death in 1816. He armed his warriors with shields and powerful stabbing spears, and began a campaign of terror, overpowering neighboring kingdoms to form a Zulu Empire.

Timeline of royal rulers

1279 BCE
Ramesses II
Egyptian pharaoh begins his 67-year reign of Egypt.

1611
Gustavus Adolphus
Swedish king comes to the throne and begins laying the foundations for the powerful modern state of Sweden.

1643
Louis XIV
Known as the Sun King, Louis XIV begins his reign, which, at seventy-two years and 100 days, is the longest of any monarch in Europe.

1740
Frederick II
Frederick the Great comes to the throne, going on to increase the military power of Prussia and become a noted patron of the arts.

1816
Shaka Zulu
Leader and military innovator takes power. A cruel tyrant, he is murdered by his half-brother in 1828.

ELIZABETH I
Powerful Queen

Late in 1558, after the death of her half-sister Mary, Elizabeth I took the English throne. Shrewd, intelligent, and ruthless, she soon established herself as one of England's greatest rulers, and her forty-five year reign is seen as a golden age in English history.

Life and death

Elizabeth was born in Greenwich, London, on September 7, 1533. She was the daughter of the great Tudor king, Henry VIII, and his second wife, Anne Boleyn. When Elizabeth was two years old, her mother was beheaded on the orders of her father. Elizabeth was sent away from court and brought up by tutors and governesses at Hatfield House in Hertfordshire.

In 1553, Mary I became queen. During the reign of Henry VIII, England had broken away from the Catholic church. Mary, a devout Catholic, worked hard, and often ruthlessly, to make the country Catholic again. Protestants were often persecuted and killed. Elizabeth herself was imprisoned in the Tower of London on suspicion of leading a Protestant rebellion.

Learning to be queen

After two months in the Tower, Elizabeth was released. Mary sent her away from London to live in Woodstock, near Oxford, but kept her under guard. She was later allowed to move back to Hatfield House, where she had spent her childhood. It was here that Elizabeth heard of her sister's death on November 17, 1558. Elizabeth was now queen at only 25 years old. A week later, she returned to London to begin the task of ruling England.

Elizabeth's top priority was to make England a Protestant country again, while still allowing some of the old Catholic traditions to continue. She also appointed a group of trusted advisors to help her during her rule.

ELIZABETH'S ARMADA DIARY

January 15, 1559
Westminster Abbey, London

Today was the best day of my life—I was crowned Queen of England in Westminster Abbey. I had a fabulous new robe to wear, and as the Bishop placed the crown on my head, trumpets sounded. I can't believe I'm Queen of England! What a day!

February 8, 1587
Fotheringay Castle, Northamptonshire

I've been so busy ruling (and trying not to get married) that I haven't had time to write, but today has been dreadful. Mary, Queen of Scots, my cousin, was executed on my orders. But I didn't really want her to be killed. She'd become too dangerous—Philip of Spain and the Catholics were plotting to kill me and put her on my throne—so I didn't really have much choice. In the end, I had to listen to my advisors.

July 19, 1588
Cornwall, southeast England
That fool Philip has sent an armada, a fleet of ships—130 of them!—to attack England and pay me back for Mary's death. The ships were spotted off the coast, and beacons lit along the clifftops sent the news to London. He's not going to get away with this.

July 28, 1588
Calais, France
Brilliant news. The Spanish were anchored off Calais when Sir Francis Drake had an idea. He ordered eight old ships to be filled with wood, tar, and gunpowder. These were set on fire and sent off towards the Spanish ships. In a panic, the Spanish scattered, and our warships were able to strike. That'll teach them.

August 9, 1588
Tilbury, London
I thought our forces needed a bit of encouragement, so I went to Tilbury and gave a stirring speech. It was pretty good, if I say so myself. Even as I was speaking, the Spanish ships were battling their way through storms off Scotland. They won't be back in a hurry. We've won—hurray!

COMMANDING QUEENS

Many powerful queens were loved by their subjects. During her reign, Elizabeth was known as the "Virgin Queen" because she chose not to marry, saying that she was married to her country.

British and Armada ships

After the Armada

The failure of the Spanish Armada was a great victory for Elizabeth, but the following years saw economic problems for England. Elizabeth died in 1603. She was the last of the Tudor monarchs.

Empress Wu Zetian

Wu Zetian married Emperor Gaozong and took control after his death in 683 CE. In 690, she became the first and only female Empress of China. During her peaceful and prosperous reign, she cut taxes and improved wages.

Empress Wu Zetian

Hermitage Museum, Russia, founded by Catherine the Great

Catherine the Great

Catherine became Empress of Russia when her husband, Grand Duke Peter, was overthrown in 1762. Under her rule, she expanded Russia's empire and continued the process of modernization that was started by Peter the Great. She loved literature and education.

Timeline of female rulers

1478 BCE
Hatshepsut
Crowned Queen of Egypt and
reigns for more than twenty years.

690 CE
Empress Wu Zetian
Becomes the first female Empress of China.

1588
Elizabeth I
Celebrates victory over the Spanish Armada.

1762
Catherine the Great
Becomes Empress of Russia and
expands the country's empire.

1837
Queen Victoria
Crowned Queen of Britain and goes on to have
the longest reign of any female monarch in history.

GeOrge WasHinGton

Mr. President

Leader of the Continental Army in the American Revolution, George Washington was an amazing soldier. After a stunning victory, he turned his attention to politics, becoming the first ever president of the USA and returning to serve for a second term.

Early life

Born on February 22, 1732, in Virginia, George was the eldest of six children. His wealthy family owned tobacco plantations and hundreds of slaves. As a boy, George was taught at home by tutors, but he also learned how to grow crops, raise livestock, and look after the land.

When George was 11 years old, his father died, and he was brought up by his half-brother, Lawrence. When Lawrence died in 1752, George inherited Mount Vernon, the large family estate on the banks of the Potomac River. It was to be his home for the rest of his life.

Going to war

At that time, parts of America called the colonies were ruled by the British and French. In 1754, war broke out between them for control of the borders between their lands. George was now a major in the Virginia militia (small army), and over the next few years, he fought bravely many times and was praised for his leadership and courage. In August 1755, he was made commander of the Virginia army. He was just 23 years old.

George left the army in 1758 and returned to Mount Vernon. He got married and devoted himself to family life and the estate. But he also began to get involved with the thirteen British colonies, including Virginia, that wanted to be free from British rule. In April 1775, fighting broke out near Boston—the colonies were at war. The American Revolution had begun, and George was to play a leading role.

WASHINGTON'S WARTIME DIARY

July 1775
Cambridge, Massachusetts

Exciting times! I've been made commander in chief of the Continental Army to lead the revolt against the British. The army's made up of soldiers from all thirteen colonies, and they're a bit of a ragtag bunch. It's my job to turn them into a top fighting force—wish me luck.

December 26, 1776
Delaware River

In August, we suffered a heavy defeat at the Battle of Long Island and were forced to retreat. But things are looking up. Last

night, we braved the ice and crossed the Delaware River into New Jersey to launch a surprise attack. The British never saw us coming, and we captured almost a whole garrison. Morale is high.

October 19, 1781
Yorktown, Virginia

We've done it! The war is over and we've won! With help from the French, we attacked the British forces. The British, led by

Charles Cornwallis, held out as long as they could, but this morning they waved the white handkerchief. We've just had the ceremony of surrender. Cornwallis didn't come—he's ill, apparently. So, I asked my second-in-command to accept the sword of surrender instead of me. Two can play at that game.

April 30, 1789
New York City

The proudest day of my life! I was sworn in as the first president of the USA and took the oath of office on the balcony of Federal Hall. A huge crowd came to cheer, and there was a thirteen-gun salute. Afterward, I gave my first speech in the Senate chamber. Being called "Mr. President" is going to take some getting used to.

September 19, 1796
Philadelphia, Pennsylvania

Today, my farewell address is in the newspaper. After two terms as president, I'm retiring next year. But before I go, I wanted to write a letter to the American people, setting out my ideas for our country. I have written about how vital it is to have unity among our states, a strong government, and for people to stay true to their values and take pride in being American.

IMPORTANT PRESIDENTS

George Washington is remembered as a great soldier, a skillful politician, and a man with a deep sense of duty and patriotism. You can find out about some other notable presidents on these pages.

George Washington, 1732–97

First president

Washington helped to draw up the US Constitution, and as the first president of the United States, he established many traditions that still continue today. Two years after his 1797 retirement, he caught a chill while inspecting his farmland and died a few days later.

Thomas Jefferson

One of the Founding Fathers of the USA, Jefferson drafted the Declaration of Independence in 1776. Passionate about democracy, he was elected president in 1801. In 1803, he bought land from France, doubling the size of the USA.

Thomas Jefferson, who died in 1826

Charles de Gaulle depicted on a stamp

Charles de Gaulle

After World War I, Charles de Gaulle was promoted to leader of the French army. During World War II, he organized the resistance against German control of France. After the war, de Gaulle led the French government until 1946, and was president from 1958 until 1968.

Timeline of presidents

1789
George Washington
Becomes the first president of the United States.

1819
Thomas Jefferson
Former president of the USA
founds the University of Virginia.

1940
Charles de Gaulle
Leader of France begins organizing the Free
French movement during World War II.

1963
Jomo Kenyatta
Founding father of the Kenyan nation
leads his country to independence and
remains its leader until his death in 1978.

1991
Boris Yeltsin
Becomes first president of the Russian Federation.

NAPOLEON BONAPARTE
Empire Builder

One of the greatest military leaders in history, Napoleon Bonaparte made a name for himself during the French Revolution. He became the first emperor of France and conquered large parts of Europe before his final famous defeat at Waterloo in 1815.

Becoming a soldier

Napoleon was born on August 15, 1769, on the island of Corsica (part of France). His father, Carlo, was a lawyer at the court of King Louis XVI, and the family was reasonably wealthy and had good connections.

In 1779, Napoleon was sent to mainland France and enrolled at a military academy at Brienne-le-Château. There, he excelled at math but was teased because he spoke French with a Corsican accent. His studies completed, Napoleon won a place at the École Militaire, a top military academy in Paris, where he trained to be an artillery officer. In 1785, he became the first Corsican to graduate from the academy.

Rise to power

After graduating, Napoleon was made a second lieutenant in the French army and was later promoted to captain. This was a turbulent time in France's history. In 1792, three years after the French Revolution began, France became a republic, and a year later, King Louis XVI was executed. Napoleon seized his chance. In return for helping the new government, he was made Commander of the French army in Italy, where he forced Austria to make peace with France.

Napoleon's next campaign was not so successful. This time, he set out to conquer Egypt, but his forces were destroyed by Admiral Nelson at the Battle of the Nile in 1798. It was a blow to Napoleon's reputation, but he was not down and out for long. In 1799, he overthrew the government and became the most powerful man in France.

BONAPARTE'S EMPIRE-BUILDING DIARY

June 14, 1800
Marengo, Italy
I came back to Italy to deal with some unfinished business—those pesky Austrians had been attacking our troops again. Anyway, we showed them. They won't forget the Battle of Marengo in a hurry. True, it didn't start off well. By early afternoon, they had us on the run, but we managed to come back and launch a surprise attack of our own.

December 2, 1804
Paris, France
Just when I thought things couldn't get any better, they did! I was already First Consul of France, but today, I was crowned emperor by the Pope. Now, I'm Napoleon I. The ceremony took place in Notre Dame. I wore a splendid robe of red velvet and fur, which was so heavy it needed four men to hold it up. I also had a brand new crown made (the old one was destroyed during the Revolution).

December 2, 1805
Austerlitz, Moravia

I needed to lure the Austrians and Russians into battle, so I came up with a cunning plan. I pretended that the French Army was on its last legs, and they fell for it—hook, line, and sinker. Then our troops swept through their ranks, taking thousands of prisoners. It was my greatest victory yet. Soon, all of Europe will be mine— I mean, will belong to France.

Sometime in April 1814
On the way to Elba

A terrible day. After a few disastrous campaigns, I've been forced to abdicate. I'm being exiled to Elba, some tiny island off the coast of Italy. Apparently, I'll be in charge there and even allowed to be called Emperor. Pah! Oh well, better start planning my escape.

June 18, 1815
Waterloo, Belgium

I managed to escape from Elba in March and traveled to Paris. Wish I hadn't bothered. Today was the worst day yet. At Waterloo, we were well and truly beaten by the British, led by the Duke of

Wellington and his Prussian pals. Reckon it'll be my last battle. Wonder which horrible island they'll banish me to this time?

IMPOSING EMPERORS

Napoleon was a military genius who introduced many important reforms in France. Throughout history, empire-builders have often been gifted administrators as well as powerful personalities.

Napoleon Bonaparte, 1769–1821

The reformer

After the defeat at Waterloo, Napoleon was captured by the British and exiled to the island of St. Helena in the Atlantic ocean. He died there in 1821. His legacy is the reorganization of tax and education systems and the Napoleonic Code, a set of rules that still influences modern legal systems.

Qin Shi Huangdi

The first emperor of the Qin Dynasty, Qin Shi Huangdi oversaw many reforms and built roads and canals. After his death in 201 BCE, he was buried in a gigantic tomb protected by a vast army of life-sized terracotta warriors.

The terracotta army

Charlemagne, who died in 814 CE

Charlemagne

Charlemagne became king of the Franks in 768 CE and campaigned to extend his kingdom and spread Christianity. By 800 CE, he ruled most of western Europe. The Pope crowned him as the first emperor of the Holy Roman Empire—although he did not use the title.

Timeline of emperors

221 BCE
Qin Shi Huangdi
Conquers the Warring States to become the
first emperor of the Qin Dynasty in China.

800 CE
Charlemagne
Crowned the first emperor in western Europe
following the end of the Roman Empire in 800.

1206
Genghis Khan
Founder of the Mongol Empire begins leading the
Mongol invasions that conquer huge areas of Asia.

1556
Akbar
Becomes ruler of the Mughal Empire
and begins expansion of the empire to cover
most of the Indian subcontinent.

1815
Napoleon Bonaparte
Finally defeated at the Battle of Waterloo in Belgium.

CHAPTER 4
REBELS

Scattered throughout history are people who have stood out because they didn't fit in or conform. These rebellious spirits have led revolts against an established order that they considered unfair and worked tirelessly for people who had no rights of their own. Often these rebels turned their own lives upside down to help others, and even risked being killed.

Martin Luther

Spartacus

But all had an unwavering belief that what they were doing was right, and this inspired them to carry on, even when the going got horribly tough.

In this chapter, you can read about a gladiator who led a slave revolt, a reformer who dared to question the way people worshiped, a woman who escaped from slavery to lead other slaves to freedom, and a man who risked his life to save others from certain death.

Oskar Schindler

Harriet Tubman

SPARTACUS

Slave Leader

In the first century BCE, a daring gladiator defied the mighty Romans and escaped from his training school. He was soon joined by tens of thousands of other runaway slaves. For two years, Spartacus and his slave army kept the Romans at bay. Then their luck ran out. . . .

Early years

We know very little about who Spartacus actually was. It is thought that he came from Thrace (modern-day Bulgaria) and may once have been a soldier in the Roman Army. He was later taken prisoner, possibly for deserting his post, and was sold as a slave. Another story says that he was a prisoner of war, captured by the Romans.

Gladiator school

Because of his great strength, Spartacus was sold as a gladiator. He was sent to be trained at a ludus (gladiator school) near the town of Capua in Italy. The ludus was owned by a man called Lentulus Batiatus. Like all gladiator schools, it was strictly run, and training was tough. Most gladiators had short, brutal lives and were expected to fight only two or three times before they were killed. But they were also valuable commodities to their owners, and it was vital that they put on a good show to entertain the crowds.

There were different types of gladiators, each with different types of armor and weapons. Spartacus was a murmillo. This heavyweight fighter carried a rectangular shield and a long sword, and wore a leather belt and arm guard. He also wore a large bronze helmet with a crest and ornate grille to protect his face. We don't know how good a gladiator Spartacus really was, but we do know that one day in 73 BCE, he decided he'd had enough of ludus life. . . .

SPARTACUS'S REBEL DIARY

Sometime in 73 BCE
Capua, Italy

We've made it out—about seventy of us—but only just. The ludus guards discovered our escape plan, so we had to fight our way

out with kitchen knives. Luckily, we also found a couple of wagons loaded with armor and weapons outside, so we grabbed the lot. Anyway, we're heading for Mount Vesuvius, and I'm told hundreds of other slaves are also on their way.

Later in 73 BCE
Mount Vesuvius, Italy

Ha! That'll teach those Romans to mess with us. They sent Glaber (their military commander) and his men after us—most of the legions are away fighting, so it was the best they could do. Glaber's tactic was to sit and wait until we were starving and had to surrender. It never happened! We made some ropes from vines, climbed down the mountain, and took the Romans by surprise!

Spring 72 BCE
Mount Garganus, Italy
We spent the winter in the south, training and arming our new recruits. There are about 70,000 of us now—slaves, gladiators, you name it. We'd begun our march north when disaster struck. Crixus (one of our leaders) had gone ahead, but the Romans tracked him down and killed him and thousands of his men. So, we took our revenge. . . .

Sometime in 71 BCE
Straits of Messina
We were pushed farther south by Crassus and his legions, but I had a cunning plan. I paid some pirates to take us over to Sicily where we could get reinforcements. Dirty rotten cheats. They stole our money, then sailed off, leaving us stranded on the beach. We need to head east—and fast—before Crassus catches us.

Later in 71 BCE
Campania, Italy
That's it—we're trapped. We're surrounded by Romans—Lucullus in front, Crassus behind, and Pompey to the north. We've forced the Romans to do a merry dance over the last two years, but there's no way out for us now. The only thing left to do is turn around and fight with all our might. . . .

INSPIRING REBELS

Throughout history, brave individuals such as Spartacus have dared to challenge their masters and have inspired others to follow them. Like Spartacus, many died as a result of their actions.

A murmillo gladiator, like Spartacus

Inspired by Spartacus

Spartacus probably died in that final battle, but his body was never found. The Romans took terrible revenge on the survivors, crucifying 6,000 of them along the Appian Way from Rome to Capua. Spartacus inspired future rebels, and his story lives on in many books and films.

Toussaint Louverture

Toussaint was born into slavery on the French island colony of St. Domingue. In 1791, he helped organize a slave revolt against the French and later took control of the island. St. Domingue became the independent Republic of Haiti in 1804.

Toussaint Louverture, 1743-1803

Statue of Garibaldi in Italy

Giuseppe Garibaldi

Garibaldi became involved in a war between some of the small kingdoms that made up Italy, and he was exiled to South America. His exploits there as a guerrilla fighter made him famous. He returned to Italy in 1848 and fought in battles that eventually led to the creation of a unified Italy in 1861.

Timeline of courageous rebels

72 BCE
Spartacus
Slave leads a revolt against the Romans.

1381
Wat Tyler
Killed during his leadership of the
unsuccessful Peasants' Revolt in England.

1791
Toussaint Louverture
Organizes a revolt as leader
of the Haitian Revolution.

1857
Lakshmibai, Rani of Jhansi
Becomes a leading figure in the Indian Rebellion.

1861
Giuseppe Garibaldi
Italian patriot helps to create a united Italy.

MARTIN LUTHER
Religious Reformer

In 1517, German priest Martin Luther nailed a list onto a church door. The list of points strongly criticized the Roman Catholic Church and caused a big controversy. It sparked the "Reformation"—one of the biggest changes in the history of the Christian Church.

Early life

Born on November 10, 1483, in Eisleben, Germany, Martin was the eldest son of a copper miner. He had several brothers and sisters. Martin's father, Hans, wanted the best for his family and was determined that Martin should become a laywer. He sent Martin to a school that taught Latin and philosophy—Martin hated his time there.

In 1501, at age 19, Martin enrolled at the University of Erfurt. It was another miserable time in his life. He was made to get up at four o'clock every morning, and he found his studies boring. After receiving his degree, he signed up at the university law school, but dropped out almost immediately. He was much more interested in theology than law.

Becoming a monk

On July 2, 1505, Martin was riding back to school after a visit home. A storm broke out, and a bolt of lightning struck close by. Martin was terrified, but took his survival as a sign from God and vowed to become a monk. Two weeks later, he left law school, sold his books, and entered an Augustinian friary (monastery). Over the next few years, he devoted himself to his calling, praying, fasting, and making pilgrimages, and in 1507, he was ordained as a priest. He was offered a post at the University of Wittenberg to teach theology.

But Martin also began to question some of the practices of the Catholic Church that he thought were corrupt. He was especially angry about "indulgences." These were promises that the clergy sold to people, taking away any punishments for their sins.

MARTIN LUTHER'S REFORMATION DIARY

October 31, 1517
Wittenberg, Germany
I've written to the Bishop about the sale of indulgences. Something has got to be done. I've also sent him a copy of my "95 Theses," criticizing some of the other practices of the Church. For good measure, I've nailed another copy to the door of All Saints' Church. They won't like it, but oh well. Some friends have offered to translate them from Latin into German. Then we can get them printed so that people all over Europe can read them.

January 3, 1521
Wittenberg
Pope Leo has excommunicated (expelled) me from the Church and has banned the 95 Theses. Well, he did warn me, I suppose. He sent a letter telling me to take back some of the things I'd written, but I refused. I still stand by all of them, despite his threats. Then I set fire to the letter, in front of everyone.

April 1521
Wartburg Castle, Eisenbach

I was ordered to appear before the emperor at Worms, where they laid out copies of my writings on the table and asked me if I stood by them. I do! So, they've declared me a heretic and an outlaw. Luckily, I've still got some good friends. They've helped me to escape to Wartburg, where I'm in hiding in the castle. I have no idea how long I'll be here.

June 13, 1525
Wittenberg

A happy day. I'm back in Wittenberg, and today, Katharina and I got married. She used to be a nun, but I helped her to escape from her convent by  smuggling her out in a barrel used for storing fish. We're moving into my old monastery—it was a wedding gift!

Sometime in 1534
Wittenberg

I've spent the last few years preaching, writing, and organizing our new Church. Many people can't read Latin, so I've also translated the Bible into German, and it's being published today. It has been a long time coming—I started working on it while I was still in hiding. But if it means more people can read it, it's been worth all the hard work.

DEVOTED REFORMERS

Martin Luther changed Christianity forever when he broke away from the Roman Catholic Church. Here you can find out about other Christians who have had a major impact on their religion.

Statue of Martin Luther, Wittenberg

Luther's new church

Martin Luther's German Bible was popular and helped spread his ideas across Germany. From 1533 on, Martin was dean of theology at the University of Wittenberg, a center for the new Protestant Church. Before his death in 1546, he suffered from many (probably stress-related) illnesses.

John Calvin

Calvin was interested in the ideas of the Reformation, and in 1536, he published a statement of his Protestant beliefs. In 1538, he was forced to leave Geneva, Switzerland, because of his beliefs, but later returned to lead the city's Protestant movement.

John Calvin, 1509-64

A young Joseph Smith reading the Bible

Joseph Smith

American Joseph Smith said that he was visited by an angel called Moroni, who revealed golden plates inscribed with characters. Smith translated, and in 1830 he published these characters as the "Book of Mormon." The same year, Smith started a new church, but its members were persecuted.

Timeline of religious reformers

313 BCE
Constantine the Great
Roman Emperor issues the Edict of Milan, allowing
Christians to worship freely in the Roman Empire.

1517
Martin Luther
Protestant reformer nails his list of
protests against the Roman Catholic
Church to a church door in Wittenberg.

1536
John Calvin
French reformer becomes a leading
figure in the Protestant Reformation.

1738
John Wesley
English priest experiences a profound
spiritual experience and founds Methodism
with his brother Charles Wesley.

1830
Joseph Smith
American religious leader founds Mormonism and
the Church of Jesus Christ of Latter-day Saints.

HARRiET TUBMAN

Anti-slavery Activist

Born into slavery, Harriet Tubman made a daring escape. Then she devoted herself to rescuing other slaves—many of them friends and relatives—leading them to freedom along the "Underground Railroad," out of the clutches of the slave-catchers.

Born a slave

Harriet's parents, Ben Ross and Harriet Green, were born slaves in Dorchester County, Maryland. They were owned by different masters, but they got married in 1808 and had nine children. Harriet was born in about 1822 and was originally named Araminta, or "Minty" for short.

Harriet's mother tried hard to keep her family together, but three of her daughters were sold to a different master. She managed to save her youngest son by hiding him from the slave-traders. When Harriet was about five years old, she was hired out as a nursemaid. Her job was to look after the baby, and she was badly beaten if it woke up and cried.

Planning her escape

Over the next few years, Harriet was hired out many times to different masters. Once, she was sent to a store for supplies. Another slave had gone to the store without his owner's approval, and the slave's master demanded that Harriet help him catch the man. When Harriet refused, the master threw a heavy metal weight at her head. As a result of her injury, she suffered fits and headaches for the rest of her life.

In 1844, Harriet married a free man called John Tubman. She also changed her name to Harriet. Then, in 1849, her master died. To pay off his debts, his widow was forced to sell her slaves, including Harriet. Harriet did not wait to discover her fate. In September, she and her two brothers escaped, but her brothers had a change of heart and returned shortly after. Harriet saw them safely back, and then she set off alone. . . .

HARRIET TUBMAN'S ANTI-SLAVERY DIARY

October 1849
Philadelphia, Pennsylvania
This time I set off on my own, traveling at night to give the slave-catchers the slip. Someone gave me the names of people and places on the Underground Railroad. (It's not a real railroad—the "tracks" are safe routes for slaves, and the "stations" are safe places to stay.) Now I'm in Pennsylvania, the free state. It feels like I'm in heaven. I keep looking at my hands to make sure I'm still the same person.

Sometime in 1854
Maryland
I'm back in Maryland where I'm helping more slaves to escape. I've been back many times since I left. At first, I was terrified of being caught, but I've gotten used to it now. And I've got a revolver. This time, I bought some chickens to make it look as if I were running an errand in town. When I saw an old master, I let the chickens go, so he looked at them, not me.

October 18, 1858
Harper's Ferry, Virginia

Captain John Brown asked me to help him start a slave uprising in the south. He wanted me to recruit slaves for a raid on Harper's Ferry to capture the weapons store. But it's all gone horribly wrong. John Brown's been arrested and tried for treason, but I know he wanted the best for slaves.

January 1862
Port Royal, South Carolina

I'm here in Port Royal, helping slaves who've run away from the Civil War fighting. They're free now, but they have nowhere to go. I've also been nursing the soldiers, dressing their wounds and making medicines from roots and plants. But money's tight, so I've been making pies and root beer to sell to the troops.

June 2, 1863
Combahee River

Colonel Montgomery has been planning a raid on the Combahee River plantations to destroy the enemy supplies, and today was the day. My job was to guide three boatloads of men across so they could set fire to the farms. We also managed to rescue about 750 slaves. When they heard the boats were going back, they ran after us, clutching their belongings.

BRAVE ABOLITIONISTS

Harriet Tubman's bravery in returning time after time to the South to lead slaves to freedom was an inspiration for all abolitionists—people who spoke out against slavery.

Statue of Harriet Tubman

A long life

After the Civil War, Harriet remarried war veteran Nelson Davis (her former husband had stayed in Maryland). Despite her growing fame, Harriet remained poor—partly due to her generosity. In 1903, she donated land for the construction of a home for the elderly. She died there in 1913.

Olaudah Equiano

Born in Nigeria, Equiano was kidnapped as a child and taken to the British colony of Virginia as a slave. He taught himself to read and write, and in 1767, he bought his freedom and joined the abolitionist movement.

Former slaves in Virginia, 1862

Abraham Lincoln, 1809–1865

Abraham Lincoln

In 1863, President Lincoln issued the Emancipation Proclamation, freeing all slaves in the Confederacy (a group of southern states). This was followed by the 13th Amendment, abolishing slavery in the USA. Lincoln did not live to see the results of his work—he was assassinated in April 1865.

Timeline of anti-slavery activists

1789
Olaudah Equiano
Autobiography *The Interesting Narrative of the Life of Olaudah Equiano* is published, helping to turn British public opinion against slavery.

1833
William Wilberforce
English politician and the leader of the anti-slavery movement in Britain dies. Shortly after, slavery is abolished in the British Empire.

1849
Harriet Tubman
African-American abolitionist escapes from slavery and goes on to help many other slaves escape through the Underground Railroad.

1852
Harriet Beecher Stowe
American author and abolitionist publishes *Uncle Tom's Cabin*, a book about the impact of slavery.

1863
Abraham Lincoln
President Lincoln issues the Emancipation Proclamation, freeing all slaves in a group of southern states.

OSKAR SCHINDLER

Wartime Lifesaver

During World War II, German businessman Oskar Schindler risked his life to save hundreds of Jews working in his factories. This was extraordinary enough—but Schindler also belonged to the Nazi Party, which was determined to destroy the Jews.

Early life

Oskar was born on April 28, 1908 into a German family in Moravia (modern Czech Republic). His father, Hans, owned a farm machinery business. After school, Oskar worked for Hans and enjoyed racing motorcyles.

In 1928, Oskar married Emilie Pelzl, the daughter of a wealthy farmer. The couple lived with Oskar's parents. Shortly afterwards, Oskar left his father's business and did a variety of jobs, including managing a driving school and working in a bank. He also joined the Czech army, where he rose to the rank of Lance Corporal.

War work

In 1936, Schindler began working as a spy for the Abwehr, the Nazi intelligence service. His duties included collecting information on railways and the military as well as recruiting other spies in preparation for Nazi invasions of other countries. In 1938, the Czech government arrested him for spying and put him in prison, but he was later released. He joined the Nazi Party the following year.

Following the German invasion of Poland in autumn 1939, the Schindlers moved to Krakow. Here, Oskar continued his work for the Abwehr, helped by his wife. In Krakow, homes and businesses owned by Polish Jews had been seized by the Nazis, and Oskar was able to buy a Jewish-owned enamelware factory called Rekord Ltd. He renamed it the Deutsche Emailwarenfabrik Oskar Schindler (German Enamelware Factory Oskar Schindler), or "Emalia" for short.

SCHINDLER'S WARTIME DIARY

August 1940
Krakow, Poland
The new factory's been open for a few months, and everything's going well. We're making enamel pots and pans for the army. Let's hope it makes me lots of money in return. I've taken on a Jewish book-keeper and some Jewish workers. I'll hire some more when we get busier.

June 1942
Krakow, Poland
I'd always known that the Nazis had started sending Jews to labor camps (where they'll most likely be killed). I've managed to keep my workers safe—for now—by bribing the officials with luxury goods I've smuggled in on the black market. And the factory's started making shells and ammunition, so we can claim they're doing essential war work.

March 13, 1943
Krakow, Poland

A terrible day. The Nazis have burned down the Ghetto and killed thousands of Jews in the streets. Thousands more are being sent to the concentration camp at Plaszow. I'd heard about the plans through my contacts, so I kept my workers at the factory overnight so they'd be safe. The Nazis want to move the factory inside the camp, but I'm going to try to persuade them to let me stay put and house the Jews at the factory instead.

October 1944
Brunnlitz, Czechoslovakia

The Nazis are sending more and more Jews to the camps, so I've had to take drastic action. I've managed to get permission to move my factory to Brunnlitz, where we'll be making anti-tank grenades. I've got to make a list of the Jewish workers I want to take with me—there'll be about 1,200 in total. I don't want to think what will happen to the rest.

May 7, 1945
Brunnlitz, Czechoslovakia

Germany has surrendered! The war is nearly over. We all gathered on the factory floor to listen to Winston Churchill (the British Prime Minister) announcing the news on the radio. I don't know what will happen to me now. I'm still, officially, a member of the Nazi Party, so there's a very strong possibility I could be arrested.

DETERMINED NAZI OPPOSERS

Oskar Schindler survived the war, but many others who tried to resist the Nazis did not. You can find out here about a few of the brave people who refused to give in to the Nazi regime.

A German concentration camp

"Schindler's Jews"

After the war, Schindler was penniless—he'd spent all his money bribing the Nazis to spare his workers. But his bravery and determination had saved 1,200 lives. When he died in 1974, his funeral was attended by hundreds of "Schindler's Jews"—the people he had saved from death.

Dietrich Bonhoeffer

Bonhoeffer was a founder of a Protestant church in Germany that opposed the Nazis. He worked for the resistance, helping German Jews escape to Switzerland. He was executed in 1945—only a month before the end of the war.

Dietrich Bonhoeffer, 1906-45

Abbé Pierre, 1912-2007

Abbé Pierre

Abbé Pierre, a French priest, helped Jews to escape from Nazi-occupied France to Switzerland during World War II. Later, he began a movement, Emmaus, to help homeless people. In the winter of 1954, he made a radio broadcast on behalf of those freezing on the streets of Paris.

Timeline of lifesavers

1937
Martin Niemoller
German Lutheran pastor who opposed
the Nazis is imprisoned for his beliefs.

1941
Maximilian Kolbe
Polish Franciscan friar who sheltered thousands of
Jews from Nazi persecution volunteers to die in
place of a stranger in Auschwitz concentration camp.

1943
Dietrich Bonhoeffer
German pastor who opposed the Nazis
and worked for the resistance is arrested.

1942
Abbé Pierre
French Catholic priest and member of the resistance
helps to hide French Jews from the Nazis.

1944
Oskar Schindler
German businessman and member of the Nazi
Party composes a list of 1,200 Jews who will
work in his new factory, saving their lives.

CHAPTER 5
INNOVATORS

Discovering something new is exciting at the best of times, but especially so if the innovation (invention or discovery) has a major impact on the course of history. Some amazing discoveries like these were made accidentally. Others were the result of years of failure, success, and lots of hard work.

Leonardo da Vinci

Aristotle

The incredible innovators behind these discoveries, which still influence the way people think, live, and view the world, are not only heroes of history but also household names.

In this chapter, you can read about a Greek philosopher, an artist, inventor, and all-around genius from Italy, a scientist who figured out how we all got here, and a chemist who revolutionized healthcare.

Marie Curie

Charles Darwin

ARISTOTLE

Father of Philosophy

One of the greatest philosophers who has ever lived, Aristotle worked on a huge range of subjects, from poetry and politics to science and natural history. His ideas influenced Western ways of thinking for almost 2,000 years after his death and are still studied today.

Early days

Aristotle was born in 384 BCE in Stagira, a small town on the coast of northern Greece. His father, Nicomachus, was royal doctor to King Amyntas II of Macedonia. Little is known about Aristotle's childhood, but it seems likely that, because of his father's work, he spent time at the Macedonian court. Nicomachus died when Aristotle was just a young boy (Aristotle's mother had also died), and Aristotle's brother-in-law, Proxenus, became his guardian.

The Academy

When Aristotle turned 18, Proxenus sent him to Athens to continue his education. At that time, Athens was considered to be the academic center of the world. Aristotle entered the Academy, a school set up by the philosopher Plato. He was to stay there for the next twenty years, first as a brilliant student and later as a teacher. Subjects were not taught in set classes. Instead, students challenged each other with questions and took part in lively debates.

When Plato died in 347 BCE, it was expected that Aristotle would take over as director of the Academy, but he was not offered the post. This may have been because he had disagreed with some of Plato's philosophical ideas. Plato's nephew was appointed director instead. Bitterly disappointed, Aristotle left Athens. He headed to Asia Minor (modern day Turkey) to the court of his friend King Hermias.

ARISTOTLE'S PHILOSOPHY DIARY

About 345 BCE
Lesbos, Greece

Since I left Athens, I've been busier than ever. For a start, I got married—to Hermias's niece, Pythias. I've also been spending lots of time here on the island of Lesbos with my friend and fellow philosopher Theophrastus. He's been studying plants, and I've been studying animals, especially sea creatures. Fascinating things. I've been dissecting them to find out more (no one else is doing this, but I reckon it'll catch on).

343 BCE
Pella, Macedonia

I'm back in Macedonia for a job offer I couldn't refuse. King Philip II wanted me to start tutoring his son, Alexander. He's only 13, but he's very smart and destined for great things, I'll bet. I've already given him some tips on leadership. Anyway, it's all going well, so far, and the king's been very generous.

335 BCE
Athens, Greece

Alexander is king now and is busy conquering the world, including Athens, so it was safe for me to head back to the city. I've started my own school—the Lyceum—and I'm very busy, teaching, researching, and writing. I walk around the grounds while I'm teaching, so the students have to follow me—that keeps them on their toes.

About 330 BCE
The Lyceum, Athens

A great day! We opened our new library, and already there are thousands of scrolls on the shelves. Some of them are my own work, but there are also works by other philosophers, including Theophrastus, and some of the students' own research. I want it to become the greatest library in the world.

323 BCE
Athens, Greece

Bad news—Alexander has died. They think he had a fever, but no one's really sure. Here in Athens, there's been a lot of anti-Macedonian feeling, and it's not a very comfortable place to be. I've even been accused of not holding the gods in honor. It's a ridiculous charge, of course, but if I stay here, I'll be arrested. I've decided to flee to Chalcis (on the island of Euboea). My mother's family owns some land there, so hopefully, I'll be safe.

MIND-BLOWING PHILOSOPHERS

Like Aristotle, all of the teachers and philosophers on these pages have influenced the way other people have thought, and their ideas continue to be important today.

Statue of Aristotle in Stagira, Greece

Influential ideas

In 322 BCE, Aristotle fled to Chalcis to escape arrest and possible execution in Athens. He died later that same year. His writings were rediscovered and widely read during the Middle Ages. Aristotle's philosophy came to form the basis for Western thought for many centuries.

Confucius

As a young man, Confucius studied the Six Arts— ritual, music, archery, chariot-driving, calligraphy, and mathematics. These were considered essential in China. Later, Confucius taught the need to lead by example and with compassion.

Chinese philosopher Confucius

René Descartes, 1596–1650

René Descartes

Descartes, a French philosopher, scientist, and mathematician now known as the "Father of Modern Philosophy," refused to accept the authority of earlier philosophers such as Aristotle. He questioned everything, and his most famous saying was: "I think, therefore I exist."

Timeline of philosophers

479 BCE
Confucius
Chinese teacher, whose philosophy becomes widespread in China and beyond, dies.

335 BCE
Aristotle
Greek philosopher begins writing some of the most influential works in Western thought.

*c.*1012 CE
Avicenna
Persian philosopher and scientist, begins writing *The Canon of Medicine*. The text remains in use for centuries.

1641
René Descartes
French philosopher, scientist, and mathematician publishes *Meditations on First Philosophy*, which is still studied today.

1867
Karl Marx
German philosopher and revolutionary thinker publishes the first volume of *Das Kapital*, written with Friedrich Engels.

LEONARDO DA VINCI
All-around Genius

Leonardo da Vinci may be best known as the artist who created the mysterious *Mona Lisa*, one of the most famous paintings of all time. But he was also a talented sculptor, engineer, scientist, inventor, writer, and architect—the list goes on and on.

Early life

Leonardo was born on April 15, 1452, in Vinci, a town near Florence, Italy. His father, Piero, was a wealthy lawyer, and his mother, Caterina, was a poor farm worker. The two were not married, and Leonardo did not have a family name. His surname "da Vinci" simply means "from Vinci."

For the first few years, Leonardo lived with his mother in the small village of Anchiano. Then, he went to live with his father, stepmother, and grandparents back in Vinci. Little is known about his childhood. He probably did not go to school, but he learned some Latin, math, and geometry. He must also have shown some promise as an artist.

Budding artist

Leonardo's father was well respected in Florence society. When Leonardo was 14 years old, his father found him a place as an apprentice of the painter and sculptor, Andrea del Verrochio, in Florence. Verrochio's workshop was said to the be finest in Florence, and many other famous painters worked there. For the next six years, Leonardo learned a wide range of skills, including drawing, sculpting, carpentry, and metalwork. The workshop also produced paintings, many of which were done by Leonardo and the other trainees. Leonardo learned fast. By the time he was 20 years old, he was ready to branch out on his own.

LEONARDO'S ARTISTIC DIARY

Sometime in 1472
Florence, Italy

Great news! I've passed my apprenticeship, and I'm now a master painter. I've joined the Guild of St. Luke and even have my own workshop (thanks, Dad). But I've still been working with Verrochio on *The Baptism of Christ*. He let me paint the angel holding Jesus's robe, and it's turned out well, I reckon. In fact, Verrochio says I've done such a great job that he's giving up painting for good.

Sometime in 1497
Milan, Italy

It's finished. I can't believe it. After two years of painting, *The*

Last Supper is done. I just hope the Duke of Milan (he commissioned it) is pleased. It has been a long, hard road. Some days, I painted from dawn to dusk without stopping to eat. But then again, it does cover the whole wall of the convent dining hall, so I always knew it would be a long job.

Sometime in 1502
Cesena, Italy

I'm in Cesena, working for Cesare Borgia, Duke of Valentinois. To get the job, I had to draw a map of the town of Imola. The Duke was so impressed that he took me on as his chief engineer. He's kept me busy drawing more maps and designing a dam.

Sometime in 1504
Florence, Italy

Back in Florence, a merchant, Francesco del Giocondo, asked me to paint a portrait of his wife, Lisa. I've given her a mysterious smile and added a shadowy feel. The painting— I've called it *Mona Lisa*—is for their new home. It'll take me a few more years to finish, and by then I might not want to part with it at all.

Sometime around 1505
Florence, Italy

I've been looking at how birds fly and am designing a flying machine! I've got a few ideas. The best is the ornithopter, a machine with flapping wings where the pilot lies flat on a board. I can't wait to start building and get this beauty off the ground.

INVENTIVE GENIUSES

Leonardo da Vinci is best remembered for the *Mona Lisa* (which he never did deliver to the merchant). But like all the geniuses here, his curiosity led him toward other ideas and subjects.

Leonardo da Vinci, who died in 1519

Last years

Leonardo returned to Milan and studied anatomy, even cutting up corpses. In 1516, he went to France to work for King Francis I, spending his last years living near the king's summer palace at Amboise. As well as famous paintings, Leonardo left behind thousands of notes and drawings.

Archimedes

Archimedes devised mathematical theories still used today. Also an inventor, he designed the Archimedes screw, a machine to raise water from a lower to a higher level. In 214 BCE, he invented a new catapult to repel invaders.

Archimedes, born in Syracuse *c.*287 BCE

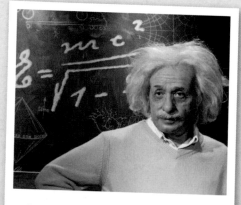

A waxwork figure of Albert Einstein

Albert Einstein

In 1905, German-born physicist Albert Einstein published four scientific papers that changed modern physics. Soon famous, he won the Nobel Prize for Physics in 1921. Later, Einstein warned US President Franklin Delano Roosevelt that the Nazis were developing a nuclear bomb.

Timeline of great thinkers

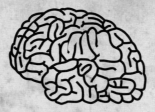

*c.*212 BCE
Archimedes
Ancient Greek mathematician, astronomer, inventor, and engineer dies after the siege of Syracuse in Sicily.

*c.*1504 CE
Leonardo da Vinci
Italian Renaissance artist paints his most famous work, *Mona Lisa.*

1687
Isaac Newton
English scientist and mathematician, a key figure in the scientific revolution, publishes *Principia,* outlining the laws of motion and gravity.

1774
Johann von Goethe
German poet, novelist, and politician publishes *The Sorrows of Young Werther.* The book makes him a celebrity.

1905
Albert Einstein
German physicist publishes four ground-breaking scientific papers and goes on to develop the theory of relativity.

CHARLES DARWIN
Life Scientist

In 1831, British naturalist Charles Darwin set off on a journey that not only changed his own life, but also transformed the way people think about the natural world. He discovered that species change over time to suit their environment.

Early life

Charles Darwin was born on February 12, 1809, in Shrewsbury, England. His father, Robert, was a wealthy doctor, and the family lived in a large house called The Mount. From a young age, Charles was much more interested in animals and nature than he was in schoolwork. Even so, in 1825, he set off for Edinburgh University to study medicine. But, he quickly realized he wasn't cut out for it. He found the lectures boring and hated the sight of blood.

Exasperated, Charles's father let him leave Edinburgh and go to Cambridge University to train as a clergyman. Charles soon got bored of that, too. He preferred to spend his time going for long walks in the countryside, collecting beetles—although he did manage to pass his degree. After university, Charles spent the summer in Wales, studying rock formations and trying to decide what to do next.

Voyage of the *Beagle*

When Charles got home, he found a letter waiting for him that would change his life. It offered him a job as a ship's naturalist on board *HMS Beagle*, which was about to set sail on a two-year voyage to chart the coastline of South America. Charles's father was appalled. His son had already dropped out of medicine, and now he was thinking about running away to sea. But Charles had his Uncle Jos (Josiah Wedgwood) on his side. Josiah thought it was a brilliant idea and persuaded Robert to let Charles go. . . .

CHARLES'S EVOLUTION DIARY

January 18, 1832
Cape Verde Islands
Dry land at last! I'm so relieved. We set off from Plymouth three weeks ago, and I've been seasick ever since. Also, I'm sharing a cabin with Captain Fitzroy, and it's a very small space. Anyway, things are looking up. I've had a fantastic few days exploring the islands and collecting samples of rocks, plants, and animals, including a couple of octopuses that keep changing color—how amazing is that?

April 26, 1832
Botafogo, Brazil
We're here in Brazil, and I've moved into a little cottage in Botafogo, near Rio de Janeiro. I've spent every day exploring the rainforest. It's packed with more animals and plants than I've ever seen in my life—it's like heaven on Earth to me! I've seen howler monkeys, sloths, and caimans, and in one day alone, I collected SIXTY-EIGHT species of beetle!

September 25, 1832
Punta Alta, Argentina
What a day! I was wandering along the beach when I noticed something sticking out of the cliff. I set to work with my pickax and soon had a great pile of fossil bones and teeth. They must have belonged to some big, and I mean GIGANTIC, prehistoric animals. I've also dug out a massive rhino skull and some bones from a giant sloth. The question is, how am I going to get all this back on board?

August 1834
Valparaiso, Chile
I've been riding and hiking in the Andes Mountains (I got my walking boots sent over from England). There's so much to see. On one mountain slope, I spotted a band of fossil seashells. How on Earth did they get here? Clearly, these mountains must once have been under the sea. I'm going to have to investigate.

October 20, 1835
Galápagos Islands, Ecuador
What an extraordinary place. It's full of amazing animals you don't find anywhere else, but it's the finches that really fascinate me. Each island has its own kind, with slightly different-shaped beaks. They must have started off the same, but gradually evolved different beaks for eating different types of food. That way, there's less competition for food.

SUPER SCIENTISTS

Like Darwin, all of the scientists on these pages spent many years researching and making observations before coming up with their ground-breaking ideas and discoveries.

Statue of Darwin, who died in 1882

Natural selection

Charles Darwin returned to England in 1836 and wrote about his amazing expedition. He realized that the species that adapted to their environment survived, while those that didn't died off. He developed his theory of natural selection for twenty years before announcing it in 1858.

Gregor Mendel

From 1856 to 1863, Mendel studied plants and flowers, noting how color, size, and shape were passed down from one generation to another. In the 1900s, scientists realized the importance of Mendel's research to genetics.

Austrian naturalist Gregor Mendel

Alexander Fleming, born in 1881

Alexander Fleming

After a holiday, Scottish scientist Alexander Fleming returned to his laboratory to find a strange mold growing in a dish containing germs. The mold had destroyed the germs around it. He named it penicillin. One of the first antibiotics to be discovered, it has since saved millions of lives.

Timeline of life scientists

1799
Alexander von Humboldt
Prussian geographer and explorer begins his travels in Central and South America, gathering huge amounts of information.

1859
Charles Darwin
British naturalist publishes *On the Origin of Species*, detailing his theory of natural selection.

1863
Louis Pasteur
French chemist invents the process of pasteurization. In 1881, he develops vaccines against anthrax, and in 1885, against rabies.

1866
Gregor Mendel
Founder of the modern science of genetics publishes his findings.

1928
Alexander Fleming
Medical scientist discovers penicillin, one of the first antibiotics.

MARIE CURIE
Brilliant Mind

As a woman, Marie Curie had to work hard to prove herself, but she became one of the most famous scientists in the world. At the end of the nineteenth century, she discovered a brand-new chemical element— radium. The discovery changed the path of science.

Early life

Marie Sklodowska was born on November 7, 1867, in Warsaw, Poland, the youngest of five children. Both of Marie's parents were teachers. Her mother was the head of the boarding school where the family lived. When Marie was 10 years old, her mother died. Marie was devastated and hid her feelings by burying herself in her books. She read everything she could find—adventure stories, poetry, and her father's science books.

At school, Marie was a brilliant pupil. In 1883, she graduated from high school at the top of her class with a gold medal for outstanding achievement. Marie and her sister, Bronya, longed to continue studying, but Warsaw University did not take girls as students. Marie came up with a plan. With their savings, the sisters would send Bronya to Paris, France, to study medicine. Then, when she qualified as a doctor, she would send for Marie.

Paris and Pierre

In 1891, Marie finally left for Paris and the Sorbonne University. She took her studies very seriously, and just two years later, she gained a degree in physics. The following year, she earned a degree in mathematics.

At the same time, Marie met Pierre Curie, a lecturer at the School of Physics and Chemistry. The two were married on July 26, 1895. Afterward, Marie began studying for her Doctor of Science by investigating the mysterious rays given off by the metal uranium.

MARIE'S CHEMISTRY DIARY

December 26, 1898
Paris, France
We've been working away in our laboratory (a leaky shed), analyzing lumps of pitchblende (a type of rock). We knew it contained uranium, but the rays were so strong, we reckoned there must be something else. Back in July, we discovered a new chemical element, which we called polonium, after Poland. And today, we've discovered a second—radium. Now we want a sample, and for that we'll need tons of pitchblende.

December 1903
Paris, France
What a year it's been. In June, I gained my Doctor of Science, so I'm now Dr. Curie! And, a few days ago, we heard the news that we (together with Henri Becquerel) have been awarded the Nobel Prize in Physics. I'm the first woman to win. We're not going to Stockholm for the presentation—we're too busy with our work. But we'll use the money to hire a lab assistant, as we've never had one before.

May 1906
Paris, France

I don't know how to write this. My heart is broken. On April 19, Pierre was crossing the road and was killed by a horse-drawn wagon. The university has offered me Pierre's old job as Professor of Physics, and I've accepted it as a tribute to him. I began my first lecture in exactly the same place that Pierre finished his. . . .

December 1911
Stockholm, Sweden

I've been awarded another Nobel Prize, this time in Chemistry. I'm the first person ever to win two, I'm told. This time, I'm going to Stockholm to receive the prize. And I'm going to use any influence I have to persuade the government to support my new Radium Institute where we can carry out research. Then I'm going to have a rest—I'm completely worn out.

August 1914
Paris, France

I'm delighted to say that the Radium Institute is now open on a street that has been newly renamed Rue Pierre-Curie. He would have been so proud. Sadly, we are also at war, so I've volunteered for war work. My daughter Irène and I are filling vans with mobile X-ray machines so that we can reach wounded soldiers on the battlefield. They've been nicknamed *petites Curies* ("little Curies").

AMAZING MINDS

Marie Curie's amazing mind made her the only woman to win Nobel prizes in two different fields (physics and chemistry). Here are other people with brilliant minds.

Polish-French physicist Marie Curie

Leading lady

After the war, Marie continued work at her Radium Institute, unaware that the exposure to radiation was slowly killing her—the dangers were not known at the time. She died in 1934, having laid the foundations for innovations such as nuclear power and some cancer treatments.

Galileo Galilei

When Galileo heard about the invention of the first telescope, he built a more powerful version and took up astronomy. But he was accused of heresy after supporting the theory that the Sun (not Earth) was at the Universe's center.

Galileo Galilei, 1564-1642

Alan Turing, 1912-1954

Alan Turing

Turing studied math at Cambridge University. There, he developed the Turing machine—the basis of the modern computer. During World War II, he worked at Bletchley Park, the ultra-secret code-breaking center. After the war, he continued his work on early computers and artificial intelligence.

Timeline of incredible scientists

1609
Johannes Kepler
German mathematician and astronomer publishes *New Astronomy*, about the motion of planets around the Sun.

1638
Galileo Galilei
Italian mathematician, scientist, and astronomer publishes *Discourses Concerning Two New Sciences* while under house arrest.

1898
Marie Curie
Scientist discovers radium while investigating radioactivity with her husband Pierre.

1939
Alan Turing
British mathematician begins code-breaking at Bletchley Park. His work during World War II (1939-1945) helps to save lives and shorten the war.

1988
Stephen Hawking
British physicist and cosmologist, known for his work on black holes and quantum mechanics, publishes *A Brief History of Time*, which becomes a bestseller.

CHAPTER 6
TRAILBLAZERS

Some of the greatest heroes of history have been men and women who risked their lives to bring about important changes in society. They saw that people were being treated unfairly, but that those people often had no voice of their own with which to protest.

Emmeline
Pankhurst

Mahatma
Gandhi

By bringing social issues to the forefront, these heroes have changed the course of history. But it wasn't easy. Often, they were treated as dangerous rebels, bent on destroying the way things were usually done.

Sometimes, they fell on the wrong side of the law. Nevertheless, they fought on, shaking up society and blazing trails for millions of others to follow.

Franklin D. Roosevelt

Martin Luther King Jr.

EmMeLiNe PaNKHuRsT
Votes for Women

Today, we take voting in elections for granted, but until the early twentieth century, women in Britain did not have the right to vote. The law was changed thanks to the efforts of a group of women, the suffragettes, led by the extraordinary Emmeline Pankhurst.

Early days

Emmeline Goulden was born on July 14, 1858, in Manchester, England. Her family had a long tradition of being involved in politics and social reform. Her father served on the local town council, and the children were often included in their parents' political activities.

As a child, Emmeline loved reading, but her parents did not believe in sending their daughters to school. They thought that girls should learn how to be good wives and mothers instead. When she was 14, Emmeline went with her mother to a meeting about women's suffrage (voting rights). She was hooked. A year later, she enrolled at a school in Paris where she studied chemistry and accountancy, as well as traditional skills such as sewing.

Marriage and politics

In 1879, Emmeline married Richard Pankhurst, a lawyer and supporter of women's suffrage. Despite a growing family, Emmeline still found time for politics and joined the Women's Suffrage Society.

In 1886, the Pankhursts moved to London, where their house became a gathering place for political activists. In 1889, the Women's Franchise League held its first meeting there, calling for equal rights for women. But the family was also struggling financially, and in 1893, they moved back to Manchester. Emmeline continued her political work, but tragedy struck when Richard fell ill and died. As head of the family, Emmeline was more determined than ever to fight for women's rights.

EMMELINE'S VOTE-WINNING DIARY

October 10, 1903
Manchester, England
We've had years of promises about women's rights, but still nothing is getting done. We need action, not words, to win the vote. So, with a few others, I've formed the Women's Social and Political Union (WSPU). We're planning to hold rallies and protests outside Parliament— whatever it takes. They're calling us "suffragettes," and we're here to stay.

June 1908
London, England
Quite a few of us have been arrested. We held a big rally to demand votes for women, but the government took no notice. So we marched to Downing Street and threw stones at the Prime Minister's house. Something had to be done. They've sent me to Holloway Prison. It's not too bad, but I have to wear this hideous dress with arrows all over it.

April 1912
London, England

We called a truce while MPs (Members of Parliament) tried to negotiate another bill. But it didn't pass and we're back to square one. We launched a new campaign, smashing shop windows to get ourselves noticed. I was arrested and sentenced to nine months in prison (Holloway again). I'm going on hunger strike to fight for better conditions for the other prisoners. They're threatening to force-feed me—I'd like to see them try.

June 14, 1913
London, England

A very sad day. It's the funeral of one of our members, Emily Davison, who died last week. On June 4, she stepped on to Epsom racetrack to get attention for

our cause. But she was knocked down by the king's horse, suffered terrible injuries, and died later. Thousands of suffragettes are here to say goodbye, and thousands more people are lining the streets.

August 1914
London, England

We're at war. Christabel (my daughter) and I have persuaded the WSPU to stop political activities until the fighting is over. The government's going to need all the help it can get. In return, they've released all suffragettes from prison. Now, we're planning a rally to demand the right to work for the war effort. We want women to be allowed to do jobs traditionally done by men.

UNSTOPPABLE WOMEN

These brave women have fought for the rights of women in many different parts of the world. Like Emmeline Pankhurst, some suffered imprisonment and violence for speaking out.

Emmeline Pankhurst, 1858–1928

The right to vote

During World War I, Pankhurst called off the suffragette campaign to help the war effort. She encouraged women to take jobs in industry to allow men to go and fight. In 1928, just a couple of weeks after Emmeline's death, women in the UK were given equal voting rights with men.

Susan B. Anthony

Anthony was a campaigner from an early age, at first against slavery. In 1869, she co-founded the National Woman Suffrage Association. In 1920, the 19th Amendment was passed, giving American women the right to vote.

Susan B. Anthony, 1820–1906

Malala Yousafzai, born in 1997

Malala Yousafzai

In 2009, Pakistani activist Malala began to write a blog about life under the rule of the Taliban, an extremist Islamic group. She spoke out about the closure of girls' schools. In 2012, a Taliban gunman shot Malala in the head on her school bus. She survived and continues to promote women's rights.

Timeline of women's rights campaigners

1792
Mary Wollstonecraft
English writer, intellectual, and advocate of women's rights publishes *A Vindication of the Rights of Woman.*

1869
Elizabeth Cady Stanton
American social reformer and campaigner for women's suffrage forms the National Woman Suffrage Association with Susan B. Anthony.

1872
Susan B. Anthony
American social reformer and campaigner for women's suffrage is arrested for attempting to vote in the presidential election.

1903
Emmeline Pankhurst
British suffragette founds the Women's Social and Political Union to fight for the vote for women.

2014
Malala Yousafzai
Pakistani activist for female education who stood up to the Taliban becomes the youngest person ever to receive the Nobel Peace Prize.

MAHATMA GANDHI
Peaceful Protestor

Called "Mahatma," or "great soul," Gandhi was trained as a lawyer, but went on to lead India in its struggle to be free from British rule. To achieve this, he used peaceful, nonviolent protest, a tactic that has since inspired freedom fighters all around the world.

Early life

Mohandas Gandhi was born in Porbandar, India, on October 2, 1869. At that time, India was ruled by the British, but some parts were still governed by maharajahs (princes) who were loyal to Britain. Mohandas's father, Karamchand, served as Chief Minister to the Prince of Porbandar.

Mohandas did not do very well at school, though he worked hard. He was smaller than his friends, hated sports, and was very shy. At the age of 13, according to the custom of the time, he was married to Kasturbai Kapadia. The couple had four sons, and their marriage lasted for sixty-two years.

Becoming a lawyer

In 1888, Mohandas left his family and sailed to Britain to study law. He tried hard to fit into English society, wearing a stylish suit and a top hat. In July 1891, he passed his final exams and went home to India, but his attempt to become a lawyer failed because he was too shy to speak in court. In 1893, he eagerly accepted a job in South Africa.

In South Africa, Gandhi championed the cause of Indian workers. At that time, non-white people in South Africa were treated very badly and had very few rights. Gandhi himself was thrown off a train for traveling in first class. In 1906, the government ordered all Indians to register or face prison. Gandhi called a mass protest meeting and launched his first nonviolent campaign. He urged Indians to defy the law, without using violence. He called this *satyagraha*, or "truth-force."

GANDHI'S FREEDOM DIARY

December 1921
Delhi, India
Good news. The Indian National Congress Party has decided to back me in my goal for Swaraj (home rule for India). They've also accepted the policy of noncooperation. This means we won't fight the British; we just won't do what they say. First, we're going to boycott British goods, such as clothes, and make our own instead. I've got my own spinning wheel and have started spinning—it gives me a chance to sit and think.

March 1922
Ahmedabad, India
Last month, in Uttar Pradesh, a protest turned violent, and the police opened fire. Then the crowd set the police station on fire. In total, twenty-six people died. This was the last thing we wanted, so we've called the noncooperation movement off. I went on a five-day fast as penance, but now I've been arrested and sentenced to six years in jail.

April 6, 1930
Dandi, Gujarat

We've done it! We've begun our protest. This morning, I bathed in the sea, and then I picked up a fragment of salt from the shore. It's to show the British that they can't be the only ones to buy and sell salt (despite their Salt Act, banning Indians from collecting or selling it). I set out from home in Ahmedabad three weeks ago with seventy-eight others to march here to the sea, 228 miles away.

August 9, 1942
Bombay, India

Yesterday, we (the Congress Party and I) launched the "Quit India" campaign. We've tried negotiating with the British to no effect, and we want them out. We want an independent and united India—now! Not surprisingly, I and many other Congress leaders have been arrested (again) for anti-British activities. They can throw us into prison, but they won't change our minds.

August 15, 1947
Calcutta, India

At midnight today, India became independent. I should be happy—we've worked for this for so long. Instead, I'm here in Calcutta while the others celebrate in Delhi. I can't join in. India is free, true, but it's been split into two countries—Hindu India and Muslim Pakistan—with terrible violence and loss of life. All I can do is pray for peace.

PEACEFUL PROTESTORS

Mahatma Gandhi's example of nonviolent protest has been a powerful inspiration for many other people in countries all around the world.

Independence campaigner, Mahatma Gandhi

A violent end

Gandhi was horrified by the violence caused by India's partition (dividing up) after independence. He traveled to rioting areas to try to stop the Hindu-Muslim conflict. On January 30, 1948, he was shot dead by a Hindu fanatic. He was mourned in India and around the world.

Rosa Parks

In Alabama, African-Americans could not use the same schools, shops, or restaurants as white Americans. In 1955, Parks refused to give her bus seat to a white person. After her protest, segregation on public transport was abolished.

Rosa Parks, 1913-2005

Aung San Suu Kyi, born in 1945

Aung San Suu Kyi

In 1988, Aung San Suu Kyi became involved in widespread protests against Burma's military government, and in 1989, she was put under house arrest. In 1991, she was awarded the Nobel Peace Prize for her continued efforts to bring about democracy. She was released in 2010.

Timeline of protestors

1930
Mahatma Gandhi
Indian leader of the independence
movement leads the Salt March.

1955
Rosa Parks
US civil rights activist refuses to give up her
seat on a bus to a white passenger, sparking a
boycott of buses in Montgomery, Alabama.

1955
Thich Nhat Hanh
Vietnamese Zen Buddhist monk and peace
activist founds the Engaged Buddhism
movement at the start of the Vietnam war.

1991
Aung San Suu Kyi
Burmese politician is awarded the Nobel Peace
Prize while under house arrest in Burma.

2004
Wangarai Maathai
Kenyan environmental and political activist who founded the
Green Belt Movement is awarded the Nobel Peace Prize.

FRANKLIN D. ROOSEVELT

Social Reformer

The only US president to be elected to office four times, Franklin Delano Roosevelt (FDR) came to power in 1933. He led the United States through the Great Depression and into World War II, putting into practice a series of social reforms called the New Deal.

Early life

Franklin was born in Hyde Park, New York, on January 30, 1882. His father, James, was a wealthy businessman, and Franklin enjoyed a privileged upbringing. From a young age, he learned to ride, shoot, row, and play tennis, and he also went on regular trips to Europe.

When he was 14, Franklin was sent to boarding school. He was not a particularly brilliant student, but he listened to his headmaster who encouraged the students to enter public service and help the less fortunate. After school, Franklin studied history at Harvard University, graduating in 1903. He went on to study law and set up a legal practice in New York. In 1905, he married Eleanor Roosevelt, a distant cousin.

Political beginnings

In 1911, Franklin began his political career and was elected to the New York senate, representing the Democratic party. He quickly made a name for himself, and in the 1920 general election, he ran for the post of vice president. The Democrats were heavily defeated by the Republicans, but it was a valuable experience for FDR. The following year, disaster struck. A bout of polio left him paralyzed. Afraid that this might mean the end of his career, he taught himself to walk short distances using iron leg braces and a stick. In private, though, he used a wheelchair.

FDR marked his return to politics by being elected governor of New York in 1928. It was just the base he needed from which to launch a bid for the presidency. . . .

ROOSEVELT'S REFORMING DIARY

November 1929
New York, USA
Since the stock market crashed in October, it's been a terrible time. We've plunged into an economic depression, and I don't see a way out of it any time soon. People are losing their jobs left, right, and center. I've set up a relief program in New York using state funds to try to help the unemployed. As governor, it's the least I can do.

March 4, 1933
Washington, D.C., USA
Today, I was sworn in as the 32nd president of the United States. But we're still in the grips of the Great Depression, and in my speech, I pledged to act quickly to tackle the huge problems we face. First up is the banking crisis. People have so little trust in banks, they're taking their money out and keeping it at home. We need to make sure their savings are safe.

March 9, 1933
Washington, D.C., USA

I'm calling my reforms the "New Deal." The most pressing thing is relief for people in need, so I'm getting Congress to pass a bunch of bills dealing with unemployment and giving people confidence in the banks. I've also set up the Civilian Conservation Corps (CCC). The plan is to hire 250,000 out-of-work men to plant trees, drain swamps, and so on.

November 3, 1936
Washington, D.C., USA

I've been elected again by a landslide (only two states didn't vote for me). So it's back to business. I'll carry on pushing the New Deal forwards, and I've asked Congress

for more aid. I'm also starting to make plans for new building projects across the country to get people investing again.

December 8, 1941
Washington, D.C., USA

My third term. I wanted to keep the United States out of World War II. My plan was that we would support the Allies by sending supplies. But all that changed yesterday. The Japanese attacked our naval base at Pearl Harbor, knocking out our fleet and killing more than 2,400 people. So, today, we had no option but to declare war. . . .

TIRELESS REFORMERS

Franklin D. Roosevelt was able to use his presidential power to push through his policies. Many other social reformers have had to fight for the changes they wanted to see.

Roosevelt on a US 10 cent coin

War leader

During World War II, Roosevelt helped to defeat Nazi Germany and the Japanese in Asia. He made plans for after the war and for the creation of the United Nations. However, the stress affected his health, and he died in April 1945, a month before the war ended in Europe.

Sojourner Truth

Sojourner Truth was born into slavery, but escaped in 1826. When she found out her son had been illegally sold to a slave owner, she went to court and won—the first time a black woman successfully challenged a white man in the US courts.

Sojourner Truth was born Isabella Baumfree

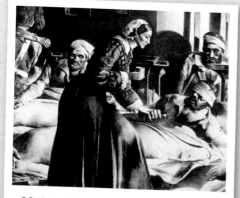
Nightingale at work in Scutari, Istanbul

Florence Nightingale

Nightingale started nursing in the 1850s. In 1854, she treated soldiers in the Crimean War. Appalled at the filthy conditions at the hospital in Scutari (in Istanbul), she set out to improve them. In 1859, she wrote *Notes on Nursing*, the first textbook for training nurses.

Timeline of reformers

1812
Elizabeth Fry
British Quaker starts to visit prisons and becomes very influential as a prison and social reformer.

1851
Sojourner Truth
American abolitionist and women's rights activist gives a famous speech on racial inequality at the Ohio Women's Rights Convention.

1860
Florence Nightingale
British nurse establishes the Nightingale Training School for Nurses and becomes known as the founder of modern nursing techniques.

1904
Helen Keller
American activist overcomes blindness and deafness to graduate from college and goes on to become a leading social reformer for deaf-blind people and other groups.

1933
Franklin D. Roosevelt
US president begins his New Deal program to provide relief and jobs during the Great Depression.

MARTIN LUTHER KING JR.
Civil Rights Campaigner

On the evening of April 4, 1968, Martin Luther King Jr. was shot dead as he stood on his motel balcony. His murder shocked the world. Only 39 years old, he had already become the greatest leader of the civil rights movement in the USA, inspiring millions of people.

Early life

Martin was born on January 15, 1929, in Atlanta, Georgia. His father, Martin Sr., was a pastor. At that time, black people were treated like second-class citizens. There was strict segregation in place in Georgia and other southern states, with separate schools, theaters, and restaurants for black and white people.

A brilliant student, Martin skipped several grades at school, and in 1944, at only 15 years old, he entered Morehouse College to study sociology. Afterwards, he went to Crozer Theological College to train as a pastor. Later, at Boston University, Martin met music student Coretta Scott. They married in July 1953. The following year, he was given the job of pastor at Dexter Baptist Church in Montgomery, Alabama.

Civil rights campaign

Montgomery was a strictly segregated city. On the city's buses, black people were allowed to sit at the back only. If the whites-only section was full, they had to give up their seats. On December 1, 1955, a black woman, Rosa Parks, refused to do this and was arrested. In reaction, black leaders called for a boycott of the buses, led by Martin. It was a huge success. In December 1956, the US Supreme Court ordered bus segregation to end.

After the bus boycott, Martin's fame spread far and wide. He became one of the best-known leaders of the civil rights movement, traveling up and down the country, organizing protests, and giving speeches the authorities could not ignore.

KING'S CIVIL RIGHTS DIARY

May 1963
Birmingham, Alabama

Thousands of young people turned up for our protest march, but then things got nasty. The police turned their fire hoses and dogs on them. Next morning, the papers were full of the shocking scenes. But today, the city's leaders met us for talks and agreed to our demands to end segregation. So, we've won the battle for Birmingham, but it was a heavy price to pay.

August 18, 1963
Washington, D.C.

Today, I gave a speech at the Lincoln Memorial in Washington, D.C. About a quarter of a million people turned up to listen. I'd written a speech, but when I saw the crowd, I tore it up and spoke from the heart. I spoke about my dream of a country where everyone was equal and where people were no longer judged by the color of their skin. I have a dream. . . .

July 2, 1964
Washington, D.C.
President Lyndon B. Johnson invited me and other civil rights leaders to the White House to witness him signing the Civil Rights Act and turning it into law. This means segregation is now illegal in public places. But the day was tinged with sadness. One of our greatest supporters, President John F. Kennedy, was shot dead in November last year.

March 25, 1965
Montgomery, Alabama
I'm here at the Alabama State Capitol, petitioning to the governor for voting rights for black people. But I'm not alone. Five days ago, more than 3,000 people set out with me to march here from Selma along

Highway 80. The governor has refused to see us so far, but as I told the marchers, I know that equal rights are not far away.

August 26, 1966
Chicago
I started the "Chicago Campaign" to highlight the plight of black people here. Many of them are desperately poor and badly paid, if they have jobs at all. I've seen how they live for myself. Mayor Richard J. Daley wouldn't listen to our demands until rioting broke out. Now, he's agreed to meet me, so I'm hoping for the best.

DETERMINED CAMPAIGNERS

Civil rights campaigners defy danger to stand up for their beliefs. Some of the activists here spent time in prison; others, like Martin Luther King Jr., paid for their beliefs with their lives.

Martin Luther King Jr., 1929–1968

The promised land

Some younger black leaders criticized Martin for his nonviolent methods, calling them ineffective. But he continued his work, opposing the Vietnam War and campaigning against poverty. In 1968 in Memphis, Tennessee, Martin was shot on his motel balcony, and died later in the hospital.

Eleanor Roosevelt

Eleanor spoke out about civil rights, women's rights, and poverty. She had her own newspaper column, and sometimes she disagreed publicly with the policies of her husband, President Franklin D. Roosevelt.

US First Lady Eleanor Roosevelt

Nelson Mandela, 1918–2013

Nelson Mandela

Nelson Mandela was involved in the civil rights movement in South Africa, helping to found the African National Congress (ANC) in 1944. After the whites-only general election in 1948, racial segregation (apartheid) became law in South Africa. Mandela protested and was arrested many times.

Timeline of equality activists

1946
Eleanor Roosevelt
US politician and activist for civil, human, and women's rights becomes the first chairperson of the UN (United Nations) Commission on Human Rights.

1963
Martin Luther King Jr.
US civil rights campaigner gives a famous speech at the March on Washington.

1965
Malcolm X
African-American human rights activist and member of the Nation of Islam, is assassinated.

1994
Nelson Mandela
South African anti-apartheid activist, who was imprisoned for twenty-seven years (1964–1990), becomes President of South Africa.

2003
Shirin Ebadi
Iranian lawyer and human rights activist is awarded the Nobel Peace Prize.

HALL OF HEROES

Sir William Marshal
Medieval knight
1147-1219

Joan of Arc
Faith fighter
1412-1431

Saigo Takamori
Samurai
1828-1877

Geronimo
Apache Attacker
1829-1909

Sir Walter Raleigh
Gold digger
1554-1618

Roald Amundsen
Polar explorer
1872-1928

Amelia Earhart
High flier
1897-1937

Walsh & Piccard
Deep-sea divers
1930- & 1922-2008

Ramesses II
Mighty king
1303-1213 BCE

Elizabeth I
Powerful queen
1533-1603

George Washington
President
1732-1799

Napoleon Bonaparte
Empire building
1769-1821

Spartacus
Slave leader
109–71 BCE

Martin Luther
Religious reformer
1483–1546

Harriet Tubman
Anti-slavery activist
1822–1913

Oskar Schindler
Wartime Lifesaver
1908–1974

Aristotle
Father of philosophy
384–322 BCE

Leonardo da Vinci
All-around genius
1452–1519

Charles Darwin
Life scientist
1809–1882

Marie Curie
Brilliant mind
1867–1934

Emmeline Pankhurst
Votes for women
1858–1928

Mahatma Gandhi
Peaceful protestor
1869–1948

Franklin Roosevelt
Social reformer
1882–1945

Martin Luther King
Civil rights
1929–1968

Timeline

1478 BCE
Hatshepsut
Queen of Egypt begins her 20-year reign.

336 BCE
Alexander the Great
Greek King and military leader comes to the throne.

212 BCE
Archimedes
Greek inventor, astonomer, and mathematician dies.

1492
Christopher Columbus
Sails across the Atlantic to the "New World."

***c.* 1504**
Leonardo Da Vinci
Paints his famous work *Mona Lisa*.

1517
Martin Luther
Displays his protest list against the Catholic Church.

1762
Catherine the Great
Empress of Russia extends the country's borders.

1789
George Washington
Becomes the first president of the United States.

1801
Thomas Jefferson
Elected third president of the United States.

1859
Charles Darwin
Publishes *On the Origin of Species*.

1860
Florence Nightingale
Founds modern nursing techniques.

1865
Karl Marx
Revolutionary thinker publishes *Das Kapital*.

1928
Amelia Earhart
Becomes the first woman to fly across the Atlantic ocean.

1930
Mahatma Gandhi
Begins nonviolent protest against the British in India.

1940
Charles de Gaulle
Organizes the Free French Movement.

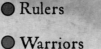
72 BCE
Spartacus
Slave leads a revolt against the Romans.

1066
William the Conquerer
Wins the Battle of Hastings and takes the English throne.

1297
William Wallace
Scottish landowner wins a victory against King Edward I.

1588
Elizabeth I
Her fleet defeats the Spanish Armada.

1638
Galileo Galilei
Publishes *Discourses Concerning Two New Sciences.*

1687
Issac Newton
Scientist and mathematician outlines the law of gravity.

1815
Napolean Bonaparte
Defeated by the British at the Battle of Waterloo.

1837
Queen Victoria
Begins the longest British reign of 63 years.

1849
Harriet Tubman
Escapes from slavery using the Underground Railroad.

1872
Susan B. Anthony
Campaigner for women's suffrage tries to cast a vote.

1898
Marie Curie
Scientific researcher discovers radium.

1903
Emmeline Pankhurst
Founds the Women's Social and Political Union.

1963
Martin Luther King Jr
Gives his famous "I Have a Dream" speech.

1994
Nelson Mandela
Becomes president of South Africa.

2014
Malala Yousafzai
Pakistani activist wins the Nobel Peace Prize.

GLOSSARY

abolitionists people who worked to bring about the end of the slave trade

academic connected to a place of learning, such as a college or university

altitude how far above sea level an object or place is

anatomy scientific study of the structure of animals and plants

antibiotics medicines, such as penicillin, used to treat bacterial infections

apartheid policy in South Africa where black and white people were kept apart

apprentice someone who works for a skilled person in order to learn a skill or trade

architect person who is trained to design buildings

astronomy scientific study of the stars, planets, and space

ballast heavy material, such as rock or stone, used to keep a ship stable

biplanes types of airplanes that have two sets of wings

boycott refusal to deal with someone or buy goods as a protest

charter formal document giving a place or person certain rights or privileges

chivalry qualities expected of a knight, such as courage, honor, and courtesy

civil rights a person's rights to be treated fairly and equally in all aspects of life

colony community formed by settlers in a country far from their homeland

commissioned when an order is placed for something, such as a work of art

commodities objects that are bought and sold to make a profit

concentration camp heavily guarded prison camp, especially in Nazi Germany

conform follow an accepted or usual way of behaving

convent building where nuns live and worship

courtier person at a royal court in the service of a king or queen

crucifying nailing to a cross and leaving to die, as punishment

crevasse deep crack in the ice of a glacier

depression time of economic hardship, with many people out of work

disinheriting take away someone's right to have your money or belongings when you die

dissecting cutting open the dead body of an animal to study the insides

evolved when a plant or animal has changed over time to survive

execution being put to death, as punishment

exile sent to live away from your home or country, as punishment

genetics study of how features are passed on through families and generations

geometry branch of mathematics, dealing with shapes, lines, and curves

ghetto part of a European city where Jewish people were forced to live

gladiator Roman slave who was trained to fight against other gladiators

guardian someone who looks after another person and their affairs

guerrilla member of a band of fighters that is not a regular army

heresy have an opinion which is against the religious beliefs of the time

heretic someone who holds an opinion against the religious beliefs of the time

hostage prisoner who may be freed in exchange for money or a pledge

imperial describing an empire, emperor, or empress

Latin language spoken in ancient Rome

legions groups of soldiers in the Roman army

medieval describing the Middle Ages, a period in history

monastery building where monks live and worship

naturalist a person interested in the study of plants and animals

oceanographer scientist who studies the seas and oceans

ordained someone who has taken holy orders and become a priest

outlaw person who is on the run from the law

pacifist someone who believes in peace, not in war or violence

penance punishment you take on yourself to make up for a wrong deed

philosopher in ancient Greece, some who was a "lover of knowledge"

pilgrimages special journeys made to places sacred to a religion

pioneering person who develops or discovers something new

plantation very large farm where crops, such as rubber and palm oil, are grown

pneumonia lung disease which causes difficulties with breathing

polio disease which can cause paralysis and muscle loss

radiation rays that are given off by some chemicals

ransom demand money or valuables in exchange for a prisoner

regent someone who rules on behalf of a king or queen

Samurai Japanese warrior

scrolls rolls of paper-like parchment or papyrus, used for writing on

scuba equipment used in deep-sea diving that supply divers with air

segregation separate different groups of people, based on color or race

siege surrounding and attacking a castle, until it surrenders

species type of animal or plant

suffragettes women who campaigned to win the right to vote for women

theology study of religion

treason betraying your country
or leader
war veteran soldier who has
fought in many wars

INDEX